Day by Day with God

Rooting women's lives in the Bible

BRF Ministries

BRF Ministries

15 The Chambers, Vineyard
Abingdon OX14 3FE
+44 (0)1865 319700 | brf.org.uk

Bible Reading Fellowship is a charity (233280)
and company limited by guarantee (301324),
registered in England and Wales

EU Authorised Representative: Easy Access System Europe –
Mustamäe tee 50, 10621 Tallinn, Estonia, **gpsr.requests@easproject.com**

ISBN 978 1 80039 500 8

Cover image by Boluwatife Olatunji on Pexels

Distributed in Australia by:
MediaCom Education Inc, PO Box 610, Unley, SA 5061
Tel: 1 800 811 311 | admin@mediacom.org.au

Distributed in New Zealand by:
Scripture Union Wholesale, PO Box 760, Wellington
Tel: 04 385 0421 | suwholesale@clear.net.nz

Acknowledgements
Scripture quotations marked with the following abbreviations are taken from the version shown. Where no abbreviation is given, the quotation is taken from the same version as the headline reference. NIV: The Holy Bible, New International Version (Anglicised edition) copyright © 1979, 1984, 2011 by Biblica. Used by permission of Hodder & Stoughton Publishers, a Hachette UK company. All rights reserved. 'NIV' is a registered trademark of Biblica. UK trademark number 1448790. TPT: The Passion Translation®. Copyright © 2017, 2018, 2020 by Passion & Fire Ministries, Inc. Used by permission. All rights reserved. **ThePassionTranslation.com.** MSG: *The Message,* copyright © 1993, 1994, 1995, 1996, 2000, 2001, 2002 by Eugene H. Peterson. Used by permission of NavPress. All rights reserved. Represented by Tyndale House Publishers, Inc. ESV: The Holy Bible, English Standard Version, published by HarperCollins Publishers, © 2001 Crossway Bibles, a division of Good News Publishers. Used by permission. All rights reserved. NLT: the *Holy Bible*, New Living Translation, copyright © 1996, 2004, 2015 by Tyndale House Foundation. Used by permission of Tyndale House Publishers, Inc., Carol Stream, Illinois 60188. All rights reserved. AMP: The Amplified Bible. Copyright © 2015 by The Lockman Foundation, La Habra, CA 90631. All rights reserved. NRSV: The New Revised Standard Version Updated Edition. Copyright © 2021 National Council of Churches of Christ in the United States of America. Used by permission. All rights reserved worldwide.

A catalogue record for this book is available from the British Library

Printed and bound in the UK by Zenith Media NP4 0DQ

Day by Day with God

Edited by **Jackie Harris** January–April 2026

Writers in this issue

Di Archer is CEO of **tastelifeuk.org**, a charity she cofounded after a family experience of eating disorders. An educator, writer and speaker, she is also resources manager on the CPAS leadership team.

Michele D. Morrison is a freelance writer, wife, mother and grandmother. She loves digging into God's word, listening for God's voice in the daily routines of life and blogging at **tearsamidthealiencorn.blogspot.com.**

Amy Boucher Pye is a London-based writer, speaker, retreat leader and spiritual director. She's the author of several books and resources and has an MA in Christian spirituality from the University of London. Find her at **amyboucherpye.com**.

Tracy Williamson lives in Kent and works with blind singer/songwriter Marilyn Baker for MBM Trust. A published author, you can connect with her at **mbm-ministries.org**.

Lyndall Bywater lives in Canterbury and works with The Salvation Army and Canterbury Diocese, helping people pray. She is the author of two books, both published by BRF Ministries: *Faith in the Making* (2018) and *Prayer in the Making* (2019).

Jenny Sanders is an international speaker, prophetic teacher and writer. She has been discipling and training Jesus-lovers for more than 30 years. She loves helping people grasp the magnificence of God's grace and the excitement of living with him at the helm.

Hannah Fytche is studying for her PhD in theology at the University of Cambridge. She has been writing for BRF Ministries since 2015, when she wrote her first book, *God's Daughters*, and has written for *Day by Day with God* since 2018.

Tanya Marlow is a lecturer in pastoral theology and a popular speaker and writer. She specialises in *narratio divina* (storytelling in biblical studies) and theologies of disability and suffering. Find her at **TanyaMarlow.com**, where you can download her first book for free.

Sandra Wheatley lives in Newcastle and loves to share God's encouragements through her writing and extensive prayer ministry. Formerly a nurse, retirement came early due to the rapid onset of MS.

Georgie Tennant is the author of *The God Who Sees You* (Kevin Mayhew, 2023) and won *The Upper Room* writing competition with BRF Ministries in 2023–24. Formerly an English teacher, she now works for the YMCA, supporting young people at risk of homelessness.

Welcome

It hardly seems a year since I introduced the first issue of 2025, and yet here we are at the beginning of another year! So much has happened in between – things we could never have imagined – and what lies ahead is unknown and unpredictable. How wonderful to know that we don't face the future alone. We can know God with us as we walk in faith and daily prayer.

We hope that these notes will help you to focus on the one who holds all things in his hands – indeed, one of our themes in this issue is all about time and what it means to entrust our times to God. We begin by thinking about what we might need to let go of in 2026, then we turn our attention to prayer before digging into Haggai's prophecy of hope for the future.

In February we focus on knowing God's love and the aforementioned study on time. We begin March with a detailed study on Isaiah 43, explore what the Bible says about tears and learn how to recognise idols in our lives. As we move into April, we consider what Jesus' description of himself as 'gentle and lowly' means for us, before reminding ourselves of how God transformed the lives of some familiar Old Testament characters. We end this issue with a study of Galatians and how we can avoid falling into the trap that was hampering the growth of the early church. This study is written by Georgie Tennant, a new contributor to *Day by Day with God*. Georgie won *The Upper Room* writing competition in 2023–24 run by BRF Ministries and says she loves writing, especially devotional articles and studies.

As I have read through this issue, I've found it fascinating to see how two or three of the same Bible passages are used in different studies. It's a reminder of how rich God's word is and how the same passage can keep revealing new truths to us.

Do let us know what you find helpful as this will guide our future planning, and please recommend *Day by Day with God* to your friends. It's lovely to hear that many people discover the notes through friends suggesting them, passing on a copy or giving them as gifts.

Let's be ready to share the hope we have and to step boldly into 2026, trusting that when God is with us, circumstances become opportunities.

Jackie

Jackie Harris, Editor

Clearing the clutter

Di Archer writes…

Welcome to this new year. As we turn to face its challenges and nurture its possibilities, we have an opportunity to set its tone. Will we step into the dawn of 2026 with faith and enthusiasm, or will we be weighed down by worries, feeling exhausted before it even begins? For most of us, I suspect the truth is somewhere between the two.

Life is a gift, but it is also challenging. It is not straightforward for anyone, no matter what our experience or our personality. It so easily gets crowded with difficulties and noise, as well as joys, fun and laughter. There is lots that demands our attention. Our heads and hearts have so much to contend with in this busy world that never seems to rest.

So, let's take this moment to breathe and have a bit of a reset.

While there is plenty in life that is beyond our control, we do have choices about how we respond. We have just celebrated the arrival of the baby boy who grew up to change the world, and nativity stories remind us that even Jesus' birth was not straightforward – his parents had trouble finding a place to stay in Bethlehem. There was no room. This is so often the problem in our busy world today. How does Jesus Christ find room in our lives among our schedules and to-do lists, our worries and fears, our joys and our celebrations? How do we make space in our heads and in our hearts?

The aim of the next few days is to give us a chance to make room for our Saviour, so that we walk into 2026 with our hand firmly in his, aware of his presence by our side. Just like a new year home declutter, we will consider whether there are things in our heads and hearts that need to go – or be replaced and updated. Some will be more relevant than others, but don't try this at home on your own. We are called to transformation (2 Corinthians 5:17), but it is never just down to us. God is always far more at work in us than we think, and his grace is enough. The apostle Paul assures us that we can be 'confident of this, that he who began a good work in you will carry it on to completion until the day of Christ Jesus' (Philippians 1:6, NIV). It's a promise.

Decluttering fear

I call on you, my God, for you will answer me... Show me the wonders of your great love, you who save by your right hand those who take refuge in you from their foes. Keep me as the apple of your eye; hide me in the shadow of your wings. (vv. 6–8, NIV)

My friend has a delightful necklace with an apple pendant on it, given to her when she became a Christian. She wears it most of the time. It means a lot to her. Her life changed completely when she started to follow Jesus, and she credits him with rescuing her from very difficult circumstances and giving her new purpose and direction. She truly believes she was looked after as the 'apple' of God's eye – a phrase that refers to the eye's pupil that is essential for vision and needs most protection.

This psalm is attributed to David, who was clearly in a dire situation, possibly when he was being hunted down by King Saul (1 Samuel 24:11). His fear was justified and very real. His life was in danger, and his future uncertain. When he was still young, the prophet Samuel had anointed David as future king (1 Samuel 16:13), but that all seemed in jeopardy now as he lived the life of an outlaw, trying to stay one step ahead of his murderous sovereign. He was desperate for God's help and protection, presenting his prayer rather like a judicial petition.

Fear comes in all shapes and sizes. It is usually linked to concern for the future, as David's was. It can take over very quickly, dominating our thoughts and emotions. It causes physical symptoms too – we may stop breathing deeply, experience tummy troubles or headaches. Being a Christian can make it worse because we add guilt to our burden. Surely, we should be able to trust God, no matter what? In case that's what you think, take comfort from David. He was clearly feeling the fear, but he didn't stop there. He took those feelings to God and then reminded himself of God's faithfulness.

It is okay to be afraid. Think of Jesus in the garden of Gethsemane (Mark 14:32–33). Both he and David knew that prayer was where to take fear. Their outlook changed because they prayed.

DI ARCHER

Decluttering bad attitudes

But now you must also rid yourselves of all such things as these: anger, rage, malice, slander, and filthy language from your lips. Do not lie to each other, since you have taken off your old self with its practices and have put on the new self, which is being renewed in knowledge in the image of its Creator. (vv. 8–10, NIV)

Ah ha. Yes, this is easier said than done, especially when we are provoked by annoying people or circumstances (children, housemates, friends, work, to-do lists…). But Paul's letter to the Colossian church leaves us in no doubt that our newly created, Jesus-following selves are to look very different to our previous selves. It sounds like the Colossians needed this reminder, for Paul does not mince his words, but he writes out of concern for them and for his fellow Christian and 'faithful minister' Epaphras. Epaphras had planted the church in Colossae and was now working hard for them (Colossians 1:6–7; 4:12). However, the fledgling community would not thrive unless the new Christians treated each other well. Paul encourages them to consciously rid themselves of bad attitudes and actions and replace them with good ones.

Paul's main reason for wanting them to change was to reflect the nature of God himself. He knew that God's Spirit brought the good stuff – 'love, joy, peace, forbearance, kindness, goodness, faithfulness, gentleness and self-control' (Galatians 5:22–23) – but they had to make room for it by emptying themselves of the bad stuff.

Let's not fool ourselves. This is not usually an overnight transition. Letting go of unhelpful attitudes seems to be a lifelong journey, but it makes sense. Uncontrolled rage, malice, slander and so on do not make for constructive relationships. Whether we need help to do this, or whether we consciously choose to ask the Holy Spirit to fill us daily with his kindness, this is decluttering that is well worth it. We will be happier for it. Making room for the power of kindness is life-bringing for everyone and can be profoundly countercultural.

Dear Father God, I really need your help with this. Even when no one else knows, you see my frustration, my poor responses and my temptations. Please help me to make room for your grace and transformation. Amen.

DI ARCHER

Decluttering judgement

For it is by grace you have been saved, through faith – and this is not from yourselves, it is the gift of God – not by works, so that no one can boast. For we are God's handiwork, created in Christ Jesus to do good works, which God prepared in advance for us to do. (vv. 8–10, NIV)

Grace, grace, all is grace. We have been saved by God's grace; we live by his grace. It's completely glorious and the most powerful force in the world. It is integral to creation and has transformed millions of lives, institutions and histories. It is freely offered, at a great cost to our astounding Saviour.

So why do we still judge ourselves as not good enough? Why do we still try to earn our place in life? Why depend on the approval of others for our self-esteem? Why look for accolades and awards to tell us we are okay?

Paul goes to great lengths in Ephesians to spell out the power of grace. First, he says it means we are accepted: 'Because of his great love for us, God, who is rich in mercy, made us alive with Christ even when we were dead in transgressions' (vv. 4–5). God has done it all for us – we cannot save ourselves, we have only to receive what has been done. Second, we are assured that our place is with him: 'God raised us up with Christ and seated us with him in the heavenly realms in Christ Jesus' (v. 6); we have a foothold in heaven. Then we are both God-made and God-designed to bring heaven to earth, in the 'good works' planned for us (v. 10).

So, on those days when life is all a bit much, and we don't know who we are or where we're going, let's take courage. God is always on our side and always has our back. The outworkings of a grace-filled life will look different for each one of us, but we are all loved and accepted just as we are, have a seat at the heavenly table and lots of good stuff to do here and now. Even the hard times can be redeemed by our amazing God. It's all grace.

Dear Father, thank you so much for the grace that you lavish upon us. Please help me to live in it today, and trust in it no matter what the day brings. Amen.

DI ARCHER

Decluttering the busyness

He says, 'Be still, and know that I am God; I will be exalted among the nations, I will be exalted in the earth.' The Lord Almighty is with us; the God of Jacob is our fortress. (vv. 10–11, NIV)

Oh my. This is one of the hardest things for me to do! I seem to be programmed to run around like the Duracell bunny, both physically and mentally. Settling down to be still and relax in God's presence is a real challenge. Add to that the pace of life with the tsunami of digital information and notifications that assault us from morning to night, and the task is even bigger.

However, I suspect that is where I am going wrong. I just called 'being still with God' a 'task', as if it is just another thing on my never-ending, never-completed lists. Whereas, when I give myself time to look at what being still actually involves, I find something rather different. For example, this invitation to 'be still' comes within the context of great threat and danger (v. 6). Compare this with Moses, who told the escaping Israelites that 'the Lord will fight for you; you need only to be still' just before guiding them across the parted waters of the Red Sea (Exodus 14:13–15). God beckons us into his presence not only in a quiet pasture, but also in the middle of tumult and disasters. It is linked, too, to occasions where his glory will be seen, and that's not to be missed.

There is no doubt that finding a quiet space to focus on our heavenly Father is irreplaceable, as Jesus himself demonstrated on a regular basis. However, it is encouraging that the stillness God offers is as much a stillness of mind and heart in the middle of the hurly-burly of life as it is of finding time outside of the busyness. I do have much to learn about both.

What is your relationship with busyness? Does it need some serious decluttering, whether of time or digital connectedness? How can you be more still this year?

DI ARCHER

Decluttering resentment

Peter turned and saw that the disciple whom Jesus loved was following them... When Peter saw him, he asked, 'Lord, what about him?' Jesus answered, 'If I want him to remain alive until I return, what is that to you? You must follow me.' (vv. 20–22, NIV)

Now here is another tricky one. Peter seems in danger of resentment, comparing himself to John, but Jesus resists his seemingly innocent query.

Let's just acknowledge that very few of us could honestly say we have not experienced resentment. Perhaps it was caused by how someone treated us or because polite requests were ignored or trampled on. Maybe it came as a result of feeling taken for granted, put upon, or having our personal boundaries continuously frustrated. Perhaps we feel our role in life, whether at work, home or in the community, does not get the recognition it deserves. Perhaps we feel others seem to get the good times, while we get the dregs.

There are plenty of examples of resentment in the Bible: Martha resenting Mary for not helping her when she was busy in the kitchen (Luke 10:40); the Ephraimites resenting Gideon for excluding them from his army (Judges 8:1); church leaders being warned against it (2 Timothy 2:24); and here, Peter is in danger of resenting John.

I have discovered a wonderful new word: comparanoia. It describes the dissatisfaction and resentment of other's lives that results from constantly comparing ourselves to others, made possible through the prevalence of social media and constant digital input. It is so easy to assume that everyone is having a good time except us. Comparanoia taps straight into our vulnerability of 'wanting more or different'.

Comparanoia sells media but traps our souls in resentment, and resentment is a dangerous emotion which leads only to disappointment and breakdown of relationships. Here, it is almost as if Jesus holds his hand up to Peter and tells him, 'No, don't go there. That way lies misery.' So, let's chuck out resentment. Could its replacement be gratitude?

Dear Father, thank you for your goodness to me. Please help me to become so secure in your love and your care of me that I don't even think of comparing myself unfavourably to others. Amen.

DI ARCHER

Decluttering stuff

'Do not store up for yourselves treasures on earth, where moths and vermin destroy, and where thieves break in and steal. But store up for yourselves treasures in heaven, where moths and vermin do not destroy… For where your treasure is, there your heart will be also.' (vv. 19–21, NIV)

What about actual clutter – physical stuff that clogs up our homes, offices or garages? For some of us, that might be a welcome problem to have because we don't own very much, but there are some basic principles that probably apply to us all. As is so often the case, they are all to do with attitude.

Whether we think we have too much or too little, what does 'stuff' mean to us? What value do we place on it? How would we feel if we lost it all? The classic question is if there was a fire, what would we try to save? That might tell us what really matters to us. It's usually the 'stuff' that is linked to people – photos or a precious memento. So, let's take Jesus' words to heart and have a good old new year declutter of the rest. Silence the voices that suggest that 'stuff' is linked to our worth. Refuse to let it have power over us. Bless someone else with our excess. Decluttering our overfilled lives has grown in popularity in the west and is thoroughly biblical.

Meanwhile, let's replace our hoarding of stuff with hoarding of real treasure that will last for eternity. Invest in the four keys to a fulfilled life: faith, family, friends and meaningful work. Jesus lived very simply, depending on the generosity of others for his itinerant ministry. We may not be called to that, but we may be called to invest in eternity by underwriting significant ministries today. Our incredible Saviour wants us to live in freedom from slavery to money, to stuff, to the pressure to own things, to the lie that the next purchase will bring contentment. It's all about where our real treasure is.

Read Matthew 16:25–27. Declutter some stuff today.

DI ARCHER

Decluttering a lack of love

On one occasion an expert in the law stood up to test Jesus. 'Teacher,' he asked, 'what must I do to inherit eternal life?'... He answered, '"Love the Lord your God with all your heart and with all your soul and with all your strength and with all your mind"; and, "Love your neighbour as yourself."' (vv. 25–27, NIV)

I am grateful that this 'expert in the law' asked Jesus this question. It was supposed to be a trick, to see whether he tied himself in Jewish law knots in answering it. The law expert cannot have been listening to Jesus' teaching for long, or he would have known that was highly unlikely. Matthew records a similar incident, where Jesus gave the same reply to the question, 'Which is the greatest commandment?' (Matthew 22:34–40).

Most preaching I have heard on Jesus' words here focus on how to love God; few talk about how to love our neighbour as ourselves. However, for many of us, this is one of the greatest lessons we learn on the Christian journey. We have been brought up to put others first, be unselfish and keep an eye on pride, but we have not learnt how to love ourselves. This makes it rather challenging to love others genuinely, including our heavenly Father. We might, unwittingly, look for payback from others to make ourselves feel better – a people-pleasing behaviour. We might put up defences because we fear being known. We might beat ourselves up for not being 'good enough'. We might find it difficult to believe in God's unlimited, radical love for us.

To declutter this lack of healthy self-love, we could consider the reminder from Jesus that we are worthy of love, just because we are God's children. We could meditate on it, turning over the words in our minds, as if we had heard them spoken. We could ask for God's help in receiving his love and grace. We don't have to be 'good' to love ourselves. We are accepted and loved by the King of Kings, just as we are. From that security, we are free to love him back and love others too.

'You have answered correctly,' Jesus replied. 'Do this and you will live' (v. 28). How can you embrace the life Jesus offers today?

DI ARCHER

Decluttering disappointment

Blessed is the one… whose delight is in the law of the Lord, and who meditates on his law day and night. That person is like a tree planted by streams of water, which yields its fruit in season and whose leaf does not wither – whatever they do prospers. (vv. 1–3, NIV)

Do you have disappointments from last year that you would rather not carry forward into 2026? Disappointments are difficult to deal with. When we feel that hopes have been unrealised or thoroughly dashed, expectations unmet, longed-for outcomes ended in nought, it is so hard to recover. The pain is real, and reorientating towards a different future is not easy.

Yet we must go on. If we want to let go of disappointment, we must first feel it and name it. The psalmist here would urge us to be gentle with ourselves. He would remind us that trees do not grow in a day. They take their time, bending with the wind until they are strong enough to stand tall. They put down ever-deeper roots to find water and nutrients to survive harsh winters and blistering summers. They become increasingly fruitful as they extend their reach, providing shade and nourishment for others.

The way for us to become like those trees is to stay close to God our Father and allow our pain and confusion to drive us deeper into his word and his presence. We need to ask for his help, to ask for specific scriptures that are relevant to us right now and will become precious to us because we come to realise that we are understood. We can find ourselves, complete with unanswered questions and bewilderment, in the living words that are in our Bibles. These are truths we can hang on to, that jump off the page and bring us seeds of new life and new hope again. Let God help you release the past and make room for his good purposes.

Read Jude 24–25. God has not finished with you. Ever. He plays the long game.

DI ARCHER

Decluttering pain

The king… had John beheaded in the prison. His head was brought in on a dish and given to the girl, who carried it to her mother. John's disciples came and took his body and buried it… When Jesus heard what had happened, he withdrew by boat privately to a solitary place. (vv. 9–13, NIV)

When our lives seem difficult, it can be tempting to accuse God of not caring, but this is not true. Jesus understands the pain of loss, because he has been there. In this passage, we read about the violent death of his beloved cousin, the man who prepared the way for him (Matthew 3:1–3). When Jesus was told about it, he went off on his own. The grief must have been overwhelming, and he needed space from everyone as it flooded in.

Jesus cried at the death of his great friend Lazarus, even though he knew that he would be raised from the dead (John 11:35). He cried over Jerusalem, because he cared so much for its inhabitants and knew the sad future that awaited them (Luke 19:41). Jesus became 'deeply distressed' in Gethsemane as he wrestled with his own future (Mark 14:32–33). Our amazing Saviour is no stranger to pain. He absolutely and literally knows how it feels.

He knows, therefore, that there is no easy answer in this life to the questions that pain raises. Decluttering pain is probably a repeating, difficult, unwelcome experience for us all. 'Decluttering' is not the right word – it is not as simple as making a choice or walking a different path. It is a visceral, soul-scouring process, for which we usually need all the help that God and others can give. So, if this is you, please reach out to trusted friends, family or professionals as soon as you feel able. Get all the support you can. Lean on Jesus, perhaps in new ways, for he truly understands. He has promised to be with you, through the thick and thin of life. You are the apple of his eye.

Read Luke 8:1–3. Healing is possible, even in the most difficult of circumstances. Ask God for it or offer to help others find it.

DI ARCHER

Decluttering anxiety

I said, 'You are my servant'; I have chosen you and have not rejected you. So do not fear, for I am with you; do not be dismayed, for I am your God. I will strengthen you and help you; I will uphold you with my righteous right hand. (vv. 9–10, NIV)

As we come to our last 'declutter', I hope you have found this series helpful. I have certainly found it challenging, but even if all of us just chuck out one unhelpful attitude and welcome a new one, based on gratitude and the fruit of the Spirit, it will be worth it.

We finish by tackling anxiety, which is a scourge for so many people. Different to worry, which is associated with specific circumstances, anxiety can hold us in its grip with a vague, stomach-clenching, mind-numbing fear about the future that refuses to let up. It can be triggered by a small event or a run of difficulties. It can affect any age, and it is notoriously tricky to shift. The world offers treatments such as cognitive behaivoural therapy and psychotherapy to try to change mindsets, which can be very helpful and seem rather like the transformation that Romans 12 recommends. We Christians, however, have an additional secret weapon: we have God on our side.

Having God on our side means we have more resources to draw on. We have a relationship with the creator of our mind-boggling universe, who promises to give us strength and help. Obviously, this does not mean that we solve anxiety any easier, but it does mean that we have eternal truths we can employ. We are not limited to human understandings but can turn to God and trust in him as well. No matter what we face in the coming year, we are chosen, made holy and cared for. God is with us and for us. He is righteous and good, and he loves us.

Read Zephaniah 3:17. Dear Father, thank you that your faithfulness to me is unchanging. Help me to keep tight hold of your hand throughout 2026. Amen.

DI ARCHER

Prayer: the air we breathe

Michele D. Morrison writes…

My favourite psalm is Psalm 63. During a period of deep sorrow and mourning, this psalm provided a spiritual lifeline to me, and I read it so often in the NIV that it became embedded in my memory. I identified with the desperate spiritual thirst of David, longing for God in 'a dry and parched land where there is no water' (v. 1).

When I wake up in the night and struggle to sleep, it is still this psalm which I pray. Recently, I found myself circling round and round verse 6: 'I think of you through the watches of the night.'

God was David's focus, even during the night. We see this with Jesus too, as prayer – interacting with his Father – was central to his disciplined life. Christians through the ages have devised prayer rituals to help maintain this discipline. Monastic traditions, for example, have devised strategies which assign different types of prayer to the eight watches of a 24-hour period. They vary in their approach to each watch, but I have found it helpful to my own prayer life to extract some of the themes from these traditions and use them to guide my own prayers.

Most of us are not able to live by a monastic cadence, and fortunately God does not work by a timetable where he is open to receive thanksgiving at one time of day or night and petition at another. However, I'm excited by what we can learn from these ancient traditions.

Over the next fortnight, we are going to build our portfolio of prayer by looking into the various approaches used by those who dedicate their lives to prayer. Although we won't adhere to the times of the watches, I find the idea of a prayer watch helpful in that it reminds me that I am not alone. I am part of a band of believers eager to deepen their love for God.

I was recently given a copy of the New Testament with the Psalms in The Passion Translation. Psalm 63, in this beautiful version, reveals the deep love and devotion David had for God. It strikes me that all effective, true prayer springs from a heart passionately seeking to deepen the relationship with our creator God. May we each approach God overflowing with praise, eager for 'the anointing of your presence [which] satisfies me like nothing else' (Psalm 63:5, TPT).

Can my life be a prayer?

Be saturated in prayer throughout each day, offering your faith-filled requests before God with overflowing gratitude. Tell him every detail of your life. (v. 6, TPT)

How can one live a life 'saturated in prayer'? With so many demands on our time – work schedules and deadlines; family responsibilities; household tasks and so on – surely only a cloistered life built around set times of quiet can be totally immersed in prayer.

It's easy to get the concept of prayer all wrong. We see it as a time set aside to lobby the Lord for ourselves and others, but in God's eyes, prayer is all about relationship. When I fell in love with my husband Don, we were both working full-time, separated by an ocean and a continent. Yet he was always on my mind. I wanted to share every joy and sorrow with him. I wanted to see his smile and hear his reaction. I wanted to know his thoughts – at a time before emails, when a letter took three or four days to get from California to Scotland.

God longs for us to long for him with the ardent desire of a true lover – to want to know his thoughts and feelings and to share ours. I fell deeper in love with Don through reading his letters. God has given us the Bible, his love-letter, as well as his Son Jesus and his Holy Spirit. As we read and learn, speak and listen, we fall deeper in love with God, and we find that he is always on our minds, whatever we are doing. And we don't have to wait a week to hear back from God, because he is not an ocean and a continent away – Jesus promises: 'I am with you always' (Matthew 28:20, NIV).

Living in constant contact with God scatters all anxieties as his peace, which confounds all human understanding, 'guards' our hearts and minds in Christ Jesus. It's a promise.

As you go about your day, ask God to fill your mind and help you meditate 'on things true, noble, reputable, authentic, compelling, gracious – the best… the beautiful… things to praise' (Philippians 4:9, MSG).

MICHELE D. MORRISON

Keep short accounts

Have mercy on me, O God, according to your unfailing love; according to your great compassion blot out my transgressions. Wash away all my iniquity and cleanse me from my sin. (vv. 1–2, NIV)

The principle of repentance is that it should be done regularly. The First Watch begins at 6.00 pm, and I've found it a good practice, at some time each evening, to be still, deliberately reviewing my day in the presence of God. His holiness reveals my sin and inspires my confession and penitence.

A few years ago, Storm Arwen brought trees down across a path I regularly enjoy walking. A woodsman had removed the heavy tree trunks but left the trail still blocked by branches thick with sharp twigs and needles. My husband Don and I took cutters and cleared the way so we could resume that particular walk. Sin, like a fallen tree, obstructs our way to God; we need his help to repent daily. Sit quietly and give God the pruners.

David's sin with Bathsheba, for which he was repenting in this psalm, is major. However, in God's sight, sin is sin – I may not have committed adultery or murder, but how has my thought-life been today? Would Jesus have walked past that homeless man? If the driving force behind my prayer is to love God more dearly and follow Jesus more nearly, then am I desperate to clear away everything that hinders my discipleship and blights my witness to the perfect life of Jesus Christ, who lives in me?

God doesn't mind where we go to find privacy and peace, but he does want us all to have times when our prayers are personal and intimate. He loves one-on-one, face-to-face meetings, for it is when nobody is watching or listening that we can be most genuine. We can laugh and cry without pretence, confess our sins, admit our struggles and be forgiven and strengthened.

If this discipline is not yet part of your routine, try to set some moments apart later today to review your day with God, asking him to highlight sin, so that you can repent and start afresh.

MICHELE D. MORRISON

My chains are gone!

Blessed is the one whose transgressions are forgiven, whose sins are covered. Blessed is the one whose sin the Lord does not count against them and in whose spirit is no deceit. (vv. 1–2, NIV)

We're continuing to focus on the prayer of repentance. In this psalm, David describes what God does for us when we come to him penitently, confessing our sins daily. God forgives our transgressions – those things we do which break his laws, for example, our harsh words, critical thoughts and selfish actions. But not only does he forgive us, he also covers our sins. God is not like we are, eager to share the sins of others and shame the sinners. There is no shame with God. As David writes in a later psalm: 'As far as the east is from the west, so far has he removed our transgressions from us' (Psalm 103:12).

Unconfessed sin bows our faces to the ground. Guilt and shame cause us to try to hide, but look at what David writes here: 'You are my hiding-place... and surround me with songs of deliverance' (v. 7). When we confess our sins to God, we find forgiveness, refuge and restoration.

Sin is a burden Jesus took upon himself on the cross. We have his promise that when we come to God in repentance, we receive his complete and utter forgiveness. We are set free from guilt and shame. Like David, we can know ourselves to be loved and forgiven and experience the joy that bubbles up from deep within.

How do we respond to this great gift? David says: 'Rejoice in the Lord and be glad... sing' (v. 11). I love *The Message* translation of this verse: 'Celebrate God. Sing together – everyone! All you honest hearts, raise the roof!' When we know God's forgiveness, we are free to serve our Lord and Saviour in joy and assurance.

Your sins are forgiven. Take a moment to meditate on those words. Why not find worship music online or on a CD and use it to sing out your gratitude to the Lord today?

MICHELE D. MORRISON

Abide

'Learn the unforced rhythms of grace. I won't lay anything heavy or ill-fitting on you. Keep company with me and you'll learn to live freely and lightly.' (v. 30, MSG)

A prayer watch can carry connotations of serious hard work. Perhaps we view it with a production mindset, feeling responsible for making things happen. It's been said that God made the world to run on prayer, which is both a delightful boost to our confidence and a weighty burden of duty.

I have particularly chosen this translation of Jesus' words, with his invitation to live freely and lightly as he did. Despite the great burdens on his shoulders, Jesus lived a balanced, joyful life. His detractors pointed out his proclivity to party, often with non-believers. He did not project the doom-and-gloom image many Pharisees showed. How did he do it, while also living a perfect, sinless life that brought great joy to his Father in heaven?

Throughout scripture, we learn that more than anything else, God longs for our company. 'Walk with me and work with me – watch how I do it,' Jesus says. In Eden, God loved to walk with Adam and Eve in the cool of the evening. In the garden of Gethsemane, Jesus just wanted his friends to be with him.

Meditation is a word popularly associated with eastern religious traditions, but it is an ancient Christian devotional practice, too. However, Christian meditation is not about repetition of a mantra, but rather a conscious immersion in a scripture, where we linger expectantly, waiting for God to speak.

'Whoever dwells in the shelter of the Most High will rest in the shadow of the Almighty' (Psalm 91:1, NIV). No life of prayer can be complete without there being a time to rest in God and simply be with him.

Lord, truly stopping with you in prayer can be so hard to do in our busy lives filled with distractions and work pressures. Help me, each day, to take time to sit in your presence, turning over your word, and listening. Amen.

MICHELE D. MORRISON

Be honest

I say to God my Rock, 'Why have you forgotten me? Why must I go about mourning, oppressed by the enemy?' My bones suffer mortal agony as my foes taunt me, saying to me all day long, 'Where is your God?' (vv. 9–10, NIV)

Sometimes our prayers can be too polite. We mask our real feelings under acceptable language, reluctant or afraid to offend God. But the Bible is full of people pouring out their honest confusion and anguish – Job, for example (Job 30:16–31), and the writer of this psalm of lament.

Lament is not a wallow in self-pity, but an honest expression of disappointment. A friend's son died young, a victim of suicide, and in her brokenness, she wailed her anguish to the Lord. When her other son turned away from the God he had worshipped, she clung to God with unanswered questions: 'Why, Lord, why?'

Up to a third of the psalms are classified as psalms of lament, many of which were written and sung by David, the man after God's own heart. In the book of Lamentations, Jeremiah advises: 'Arise, cry out in the night, as the watches of the night begin; pour out your heart like water in the presence of the Lord' (Lamentations 2:19). God does not tell us to just 'suck it up': he tells us to bring our questions and anguish to him.

In this psalm, we see that in the midst of his turmoil, the writer is desperate for God. 'My soul thirsts for God, for the living God. When can I go and meet with God?' (v. 2). The world has dealt him terrible blows, but he knows one who is greater than the prince of this world, and his psalm ends on a note of triumphant faith, even amid the heartbreak: 'Put your hope in God, for I will yet praise him, my Saviour and my God' (v. 11).

An honest prayer of lament expresses a flickering faith that God will make all things right.

If you are suffering sorrow, disappointment or loss just now, don't put on a brave face with God. Let your tears flow as you lift your heart to the Lord, who is close to the broken-hearted.

MICHELE D. MORRISON

Love your enemies

Jesus said, 'Father, forgive them, for they do not know what they are doing.' (v. 34, NIV)

Perhaps prayer is never more powerful than when it is uttered with honest concern for one's enemies. This small section of scripture is beautiful in that it presents a complete picture – Jesus' prayer breathed out for those hammering the nails into his limbs, and answered, after Jesus died, when the centurion exclaimed: 'Surely this was a righteous man' (v. 47).

Intercessory prayer is easy when we are longing for a good outcome for someone we know, love or simply see as suffering unjustly. We'll look at that tomorrow. Today we are thinking about praying for others whom we may have good reason not to like.

Our daughter recommended a film years ago – *The Last Supper* – which tells the story of a group of university students who shared a house. While speculating on how history would have been better had someone killed Hitler before he got into power, they decided to identify people with ideas that they thought dangerous and invite one for dinner each week. On the table, one of the decanters held poisoned wine, and if the guest revealed that they held ideas agreed by the group to be reprehensible, they gave the guest the poisoned chalice. They considered they were saving the world from trauma and tragedy.

Jesus would have invited that person with questionable ideas for a meal, but rather than pour them poison, he would have demonstrated and extended to them the unconditional, life-changing love of God.

I can name some world leaders I might think we're better off without. Can you think of anyone? If so, with God's help, pray the prayer of Jesus: 'Father, forgive them, for they do not know what they are doing.' I wonder how the world would look if the believing church united in such painful, powerful prayers of intercession.

Jesus said we are to love our enemies and pray for those who persecute us. As you think of victims of violence and injustice, ask God to help you to pray for Damascene-like conversions for their persecutors.

MICHELE D. MORRISON

Pray persistently from a heart of love

'Your fruit will last, because whatever you ask of my Father, for my sake, he will give it to you! So this is my parting command: Love one another deeply!' (vv. 16–17, TPT)

Intercessory prayer may focus on global leaders or family members, individuals or situations. It should be inspired by love and prayed in Jesus' name. So, what does it mean to pray in the name of Jesus? It means to 'put your life on the line for your friends' (John 15:13, MSG). We are to love one another the way Jesus loves us. Unconditionally.

How can we love unconditionally, like Jesus did, with total commitment? The writer to the Romans encourages us to be transformed by the renewal of our minds (Romans 12:2). One of my persistent prayers is for God to transform my thinking by the renewal of my mind, so that my default thoughts are the same loving thoughts as those of Jesus. It's a work in progress. I often use the words of the bridge in the worship song 'Hosanna' by Hillsong.

As the parable of the persistent widow demonstrates (Luke 18:1–8), effective prayer often requires perseverance as well as love. The renowned preacher D.L. Moody prayed every day for the salvation of 100 people. During his lifetime, 96 of them became believers, and the final four were converted at his funeral. He loved with the love of Jesus, and he persevered until the end.

Consistent, persistent prayer can be facilitated by structures such as prayer watches. One year, a friend and I committed to pray for our local secondary school every day at 10.00 am during Lent. The commitment made us accountable to each other for persevering, and we saw answers as a result.

Who is on your heart today? What is the need for which you are asking God to intervene? Be specific and persevere, keeping a prayer diary to encourage you.

MICHELE D. MORRISON

Sometimes there are no words

At times we don't even know how to pray, or know the best things to ask for. But the Holy Spirit rises up within us to super-intercede on our behalf, pleading to God with emotional sighs too deep for words. (v. 26, TPT)

Prayer, like a symphony, weaves together swelling crescendos of noisy, passionate appeal or outbursts of joy interspersed with heartbeats of silence. Sometimes the silence can be peaceful, as we rest in King Jesus. We may feel satisfied, like the weaned child on her father's knee or perhaps we experience a peaceful sense of waiting, trusting him with everything troubling us.

Sometimes, though, the silence can be uncomfortable, as if a timpani drum is whispering out a disquieting throb, causing us to squirm and fidget in an overwhelming desire to see a complicated situation resolve successfully, but struggling to know how to pray for it. When a situation is so tangled that we don't know what the right thing is to pray, the Spirit 'pleads to God with emotional sighs too deep for words'.

I am close to a Ukrainian refugee family which has been torn apart by the war there, and on top of that, the decisions of one of the parents is compounding the agony, especially for the two children. It is so complex, and I have been guilty of voicing criticism and judgement which are not mine to voice or even entertain. At last, I have fallen silent, holding them all before the throne of grace, sensing the Spirit's leading in sighs or a prayer language he gives.

I don't find this easy. I want to figure it out and see them sorted, united and happy. I am tempted to suggest my own good ideas, except that I know I have none. I struggle to focus on God as I lift them up into his presence, but I am convinced that by doing that again and again, we will see the God of miracles act. He will be glorified, and they will be saved.

God of miracles, your ways are not my ways. Focus my expectant eyes on you, that as I lift before you the complex prayer needs of those I love, I am held in your peace and confident in your love. Amen.

MICHELE D. MORRISON

A circular act of love

'I have been praying here out of my great anguish and grief.' Eli answered, 'Go in peace, and may the God of Israel grant you what you have asked of him.' (vv. 16–17, NIV)

What a woman of faith we see here! She took her heartbroken disappointment straight to God in his holy temple. She didn't bother about how she looked to others, even to the spiritual leader of her day. Her heart was heavy, and she had just one request: 'Please give me a son, Lord.'

Learning of her sincerity and faith, Eli didn't grill her for the detail of her situation; he simply stood with her in prayer and asked the God of Israel to grant her request. Eli may have messed up at other times in his priestly functions, but here we see him at his best.

Petition is the word used to describe a prayer for our own needs. While our heavenly Father knows – better than we do – what we need and desire, he loves it when we bring those petitions to him and depend on him to act. Do you hesitate to bring your own problems to God, feeling you must pray for everyone else but not yourself? God is our Father, and he longs for us to come to him.

I am aware that there may be readers who, like Hannah, have begged God for a child but have not had their prayers answered. For you, I am praying now, for peace and grace. My sister had four miscarriages and never a living baby, so I know at close hand the inner agony of such disappointment.

Hannah's answer to prayer brought a different sort of anguish to her, when she faithfully fulfilled her promise to give her precious son to the Lord in his temple. I am in awe of her.

Father, you know the deepest desires of my heart, and the distress and disappointment I carry. I lift my heart to you right now. I believe; please help my unbelief. Amen.

MICHELE D. MORRISON

In the quiet place

'But when you pray, go into your room, close the door and pray to your Father, who is unseen. Then your Father, who sees what is done in secret, will reward you.' (v. 6, NIV)

A friend told me that if she sat down on her own to pray, she usually fell asleep. She found it challenging to remain alert in prayer unless she was praying with another person. I tend to struggle to remain focused on God, often entertaining distracting thoughts which dance through my mind unbidden. These usually come from my to-do list, beckoning me to wind up and get on with my day, a thought which carries the connotation that time spent praying is unproductive.

God, however, didn't create us to be productive. He created us to be his friends. In love with us, he longs for us to love him with abandonment and passion.

The reward spoken of here is not necessarily an answer to a petition. Yes, it might be a miraculous intervention, but the reward that is most wonderful is the deeper love for God which naturally grows while spending time with him.

A setting of place can help create a prayerful atmosphere: light a candle, play soft worship music or simply, as Jesus suggests, close the door. I have a friend whose creativity leads her to collage, paint or craft as she gives time to Jesus. I've tried that, and it can be revelatory and moving. I sometimes stroke a small wooden cross from Jerusalem, anoint my forehead with oil or remove my shoes, recognising I am in a holy place with a holy God.

Some sense God's presence in the garden. Many Jesus-followers chat to God and sense his voice as they work the soil or tend the flowers. I enjoy a solitary walk in nature, where I can speak out my prayers and simply listen as I walk. I find God often draws my attention to something ordinary through which he speaks to me.

Today, set aside time and create a space to deliberately close the door to the alarms of your phone, the nudges of errands and the urges of the world. Seek God because you love him and want to love him more.

MICHELE D. MORRISON

A call to arms

Finally, be strong in the Lord and in his mighty power. Put on the full armour of God, so that you can take your stand against the devil's schemes. (vv. 10–11, NIV)

Paul turns his attention here to spiritual warfare, in which we can only prevail against the devil's schemes if we are wearing the belt of truth, the breastplate of righteousness, the shoes of the gospel of peace and the helmet of salvation, and if we are carrying the shield of faith and wielding the sword of the Spirit. Armed and ready, we can stand strong in Jesus' name.

Jesus is building his church through you and me. He calls us to partner with him in defeating the enemy for good and bringing salvation to all. This prayer is active, and we don't do it in our own strength. Rather, we rely on God through the power of his Holy Spirit, because: 'You're up against far more than you can handle on your own' (v. 13, MSG).

On the day of Pentecost, the believers were waiting prayerfully in the upper room as the ascending Jesus had instructed them. Suddenly, at 9.00 am, the house was shaken with a turbulent wind, tongues of fire came to rest on each of them and they were all filled with the Holy Spirit. Then, through the Spirit's power, they were equipped to share the good news in the languages of the visitors to Jerusalem, and they did so with enthusiasm and joy. Peter, especially, was empowered to preach with conviction and boldness.

As members of God's church, we are blessed with access to the same spiritual weaponry that the early church used so effectively. In this spiritual battle, God gives some believers words of knowledge and wisdom, some prophetic insights, some leadership qualities, some gifts of healing and miraculous powers and so on. No gift is given for personal glory: it all flows from the throne of the king and to him is all the glory, honour and praise. Go on being filled with the Spirit.

Lord Jesus, I want to be armed and ready and filled with your Holy Spirit. I am eager to meet the challenges of this day led and empowered by you. Amen.

MICHELE D. MORRISON

Raise the roof!

Praise him with the sounding of the trumpet, praise him with the harp and lyre, praise him with tambourine and dancing, praise him with the strings and pipe, praise him with the clash of cymbals. (vv. 3–5, NIV)

How do you like to praise Jesus? Some people like a resounding organ. I love modern worship songs with exuberant melodies, twanging guitars, clanging cymbals and drums driving the rhythm. In fact, it was hearing a small group of believers singing their hearts out to Jesus in melodies I'd never heard before, with passionate love in their voices, which provided the key to unlocking the door of my heart 45 years ago so Jesus could fill me with his Holy Spirit.

Praise is a powerful prayer tool, because when we sing our hearts out to God, we proclaim our absolute trust in him. We declare through faith that whatever life looks like in the world or our corner of it, we know that Jesus will be back to put all things right. The prince of peace will return to establish his kingdom here on earth, where every tear will be wiped away and there will be no more death (Revelation 21:4).

When scriptural truths are sung with love and conviction, not only is faith confirmed but also the enemy's strongholds tremble and fall.

The writer to the Hebrews says of Jesus: 'The Son is the radiance of God's glory and the exact representation of his being, sustaining all things by his powerful word' (1:3). This is who we praise and worship, the one through whom all things are created.

Psalm 149 urges us to sing for joy on our beds. My husband Don would not welcome that! I often awaken with praise in my mind though: my spirit has been singing in my sleep. Aren't you grateful for technology by which we can access so much diversity in praise music these days?

Whether you soar with a cantata by Bach or jig with a melody by Hillsong, whether you stream your music or use a CD or vinyl, make time to praise the Son of God now.

MICHELE D. MORRISON

Don't fall into temptation

Peter declared, 'Even if I have to die with you, I will never disown you.' And all the other disciples said the same... He swore to them, 'I don't know the man!' (v. 35, 74, NIV)

Jesus instructs Peter and John to keep watch and to pray (v. 41). He isn't asking his friends to pray that he won't be arrested, tried and executed: he tells them to pray so that they will not give way to the temptation to sin – and the sin to which Peter gives way spectacularly is denying his relationship with Jesus. The very thing he swore he would never do.

Oh, this is disturbingly close. In our secular world, declaring a relationship with Jesus can draw aggressive attention which most of us prefer to avoid. We maintain silence when a controversial subject or polarising public figure is discussed. Some branches of the Christian faith have become identified with extreme political views, and we may not want to be associated with those views.

Personally, I struggle not to join in bemoaning the current state of the world. Certainly, there is much to complain about and even fear: environmental ruin, rising cost of living, unethical politicians, wars and so on. As a Christian, though, I know that Jesus is coming back, and when he does, everything will be put right. I am challenged to voice optimism, hoping it might stimulate the question: 'What do you base your hope on?' From Peter, the one who denied his Saviour, comes the advice to 'always be prepared to give an answer to everyone who asks you to give the reason for the hope that you have' (1 Peter 3:15). Are you prepared?

By the way, did you notice the startling statement Jesus makes, which the disciples apparently missed? 'After I have risen, I will go ahead of you into Galilee' (v. 32). Had Peter focused on this bold declaration, hope might have overcome fear in his hour of trial.

Lord Jesus, help me focus on your promises, even in the face of the apparent realities of the day. Then give me courage and words to express my confidence in you. Amen.

MICHELE D. MORRISON

Wait and watch

I pray to God – my life a prayer – and wait for what he'll say and do. My life's on the line before God, my Lord, waiting and watching till morning, waiting and watching till morning. (vv. 5–6, MSG)

I love the beautiful cadence of the repeated phrase 'waiting and watching'. Most of us are not very good at this, but it's in the action of waiting and watching that our thanksgiving and praise are fuelled and our love for God is deepened. To the Lord, a single day is like a thousand years and a thousand years are like a single day. This truth encourages us when the answer to our prayers tarry, but a problem arises when it takes so long that we forget we ever asked! We need all the help we can get not to grow weary in waiting and just give up.

A journal is a great stimulus to prayer. Whatever method we use to record our requests, it's important to have a clear way of noting the answers. For a few years, I kept a record, specifically for the purpose of remembering my prayers without losing them in the body of prose which I might never again read. Every Thursday afternoon, I divided a blank page into thirds. Each third gave room for me to record what the Lord had done *for* me, what he'd done *in* me, and what he'd done *through* me with reference to specific prayers. I looked back at the previous week's notations and carried them forward into whichever category was now appropriate. I found often that although God didn't do for me what I had asked, in fact he had answered my request by changing something in me or someone else or a situation through me.

God is love, and he answers our prayers. He pours down his mercies and his grace on his children. He delights in us despite our persistent failings. And so, we finish our study giving thanks to the Lord, for he is good and his love endures forever.

God simply wants to spend time with you today. You could set an hourly alarm, a gentle ding, that would draw your thoughts, even momentarily, to his loving presence, which is always with you.

MICHELE D. MORRISON

Haggai: hope for the future

Amy Boucher Pye writes...

In Britain, the end of January can feel gloomy and dreary, with the long month seeming to drag on for ages after the glories of December, with its lights, laughter, presents and feasting. The weather can also contribute to a sense of dis-ease and weariness, with grey overcast skies making us feel damp and gloomy. I can almost hear some of you questioning why we are studying a little-known Old Testament prophet at such a time. 'Surely,' you say, 'this feels a January pledge taken too far.',

Despair not! Digging into the words of this ancient book in little portions can help us to focus on our priorities, a good practice in the new year. Moreover, God's message reverberates with hope, not only for the future but also for our todays. Even as God called his people in Haggai's time to notice where their focus lay – their houses instead of his house – so too can we heed the gentle and loving nudge of the Holy Spirit to return our attention to what really matters, namely loving God and our neighbour. I hope and trust that your faith will be strengthened as we work our way through this little book.

As a bit of background, Haggai acts as God's messenger to the group of God's people who had returned from Babylon, where they'd been exiled after the fall of Jerusalem. Haggai, whose name means 'feast', spoke these words two months before the prophet Zechariah gave his message, around 520–518BC, with both prophets raising God's concern that his people would return to him both emotionally and physically. Haggai addresses their malaise – when they first arrived back to the ruins of their once glorious temple, they'd experienced the early excitement of a new project, but then their energy had fizzled to apathy. They were focused on their own homes instead of rebuilding the temple.

Haggai gives a message of conviction but also hope: instead of continuing to sin, God's people can embrace God's promise that he is with them. They need not fear but can receive his peace – and they can look to the future, when he will send his Messiah to save the world.

Haggai's message is for us too.

Time to commit

'You expected much, but see, it turned out to be little. What you brought home, I blew away. Why?' declares the Lord Almighty. 'Because of my house, which remains a ruin, while each of you is busy with your own house.' (v. 9, NIV)

'These people...' says the Lord (v. 2). We can hear God's sadness as he distances himself from his people, calling them not his own but instead employing a more detached form of speech. The exiles had returned home, but the task of rebuilding the temple was big and arduous. They started off strong with this project, but after a few years, they turned their focus on to their own homes. Nearly 20 years had passed since their return, and God decides it's time to nudge them again – to call them home to him so that they would make him their top priority.

Notice how in verses 5–6 and following, God uses vivid language to emphasise their empty lifestyle. They can't find satisfaction in any of the everyday things of their lives. All their efforts feel meaningless – they toil and work, but their wages disappear in a purse mired with holes. Why? Because they've ignored God. He makes clear that only a little puff of his breath blows their efforts into dross.

This is why reading Haggai in January can be helpful for us. At the beginning of the year, we might be more open to examining our hearts and habits, to welcoming the loving conviction of the Holy Spirit to reveal to us where we, like the returned exiles, have moved away from our first love. How might we be building our own house – physically or figuratively – when God calls us to be focused on his?

You might wish to think back over the first weeks of January with God, noticing any resolutions, promises or words-for-the-year that you've chosen. Now that we're a few weeks in, how are you doing? How is God calling you to live in 2026?

Loving God, thank you that you only want what's best for me and that your call to return to you is rooted in love and the longing for me to flourish and grow. I want to live committed to you. Amen.

AMY BOUCHER PYE

God with us

And the people feared the Lord. Then Haggai, the Lord's messenger, gave this message of the Lord to the people: 'I am with you,' declares the Lord. (vv. 12–13, NIV)

When contemplating a work project or a hard conversation with a loved one or getting out of bed and going to the gym, I often think: 'I can't do this!' As I voice my complaint before God, I sense his loving words in response: 'I'm with you. Let's do it together.' And when I put my hands to keyboard or inhale before addressing the difficult situation or don my workout clothes, I find that the task before me isn't as challenging as I thought. God is with me and that makes all the difference. This is what happened to God's people at the time of Haggai.

They realise that what God says via Haggai is true – because of a lack of moisture, which is out of their hands, their crops have failed. Understanding the consequences of their actions helps them to fear the Lord and obey him. And though God grieves their faithlessness, he doesn't punish them needlessly. While showing them what their actions have led to, he gives them a promise that changes their situation completely: 'I am with you' (v. 13). He implies: 'It's all going to be okay because you have my presence. I won't leave you. The work may be hard, but we can toil together.' And so, as the Lord stirs up their spirits, they set to the task. With his help, the people undertake the work on God's house (vv. 14–15).

'I am with you', God promises. How could these four words transform your day, whatever good or challenging things you face? How can you release your fears and concerns as you embrace the transforming presence of God with you?

Jesus, Emmanuel, you are with me. Through the presence of the Holy Spirit, you dwell within me and will never leave me. Thank you for this life-changing promise of your love and faithfulness. Amen.

AMY BOUCHER PYE

Don't fear

'Be strong, all you people of the land,' declares the Lord, 'and work. For I am with you,' declares the Lord Almighty. 'This is what I covenanted with you when you came out of Egypt. And my Spirit remains among you. Do not fear.' (vv. 4–5, NIV)

True to the meaning of his name, Haggai delivers his next message to the remnant of God's people on a feast day, namely when they mark the Day of Atonement and the Feast of Tabernacles. God's people are about a month into their renewed commitment to rebuild his house, and with the memories that the feasts evoke, perhaps they're losing heart. They may be thinking back, whether through their imaginations or, if they are old enough, through their memories, to the glories of times gone by and the temple in its full majesty. As they survey the ruins and their efforts at clearing the rubbish, they get overwhelmed.

But God through Haggai intervenes. In words that will remind them of Joshua and the exile, he lovingly admonishes them to be strong and to work. He assures them he is with them – words we examined yesterday – and promises that his Spirit is with them. He reminds them of the covenant he made with them years and years ago. He is faithful; they need not fear.

How often do we need God's loving and firm reminders of his caring presence with us? I'm guessing as much as his people did long ago. Even as we survey the ruins in our lives, whether relationships or failed dreams, we might think that the work ahead is too hard. I don't only mean physical work here, but the work to believe, for this is the main work God calls us to, to know and believe that he loves us – that contrary to what we might fear, he won't leave us.

I invite you to spend a few moments receiving those promises of God: be strong; don't fear; I'm with you.

Ponder Jesus' parting words to his friends: 'Therefore go and make disciples of all nations… And surely I am with you always, to the very end of the age' (Matthew 28:19–20).

AMY BOUCHER PYE

God's peace

'The glory of this present house will be greater than the glory of the former house,' says the Lord Almighty. 'And in this place I will grant peace,' declares the Lord Almighty. (v. 9, NIV)

When we're bogged down in the 'messy middle' of a project (or a relationship), we can easily become discouraged about the long road ahead. We're not in the early stages of fun, optimism and hope; we've encountered some roadblocks and hardships that we hadn't anticipated; we fear we'll never reach the finish line. As I ponder this malaise and even despair, I think of the saying by Hudson Taylor, missionary to China: 'There are three stages in every great work of God: first, it is impossible, then it is difficult, then it is done.'

God encourages his people to keep on keeping on with the project, because he will come and 'shake the heavens and the earth' with his presence (v. 6) and fill it with his glory (v. 7). The glory of the old days, the people wonder. No, he answers in advance – glory even greater than in the former house. And not only glory, but his peace (v. 9).

God's promise of peace – the Hebrew notion of shalom, a wholehearted fullness of life – would greatly encourage his people. Shalom would be their greeting and their farewell; a hope and a promise from the one who loves them, that they in turn bestow on those they meet.

God continues to promise his peace to us, his beloved. As Paul said to the new church at Ephesus, 'peace to you who were far away and peace to those who were near' (Ephesians 2:17). How? 'Through [Jesus] we both have access to the Father by one Spirit' (Ephesians 2:18).

Whether in a messy middle, at the beginning or at the end of our circumstances, we can embrace God's peace. May you know this full-bodied shalom this day.

'The Lord bless you and keep you; the Lord make his face shine on you and be gracious to you; the Lord turn his face towards you and give you peace' (Numbers 6:22–26).

AMY BOUCHER PYE

Holy or defiled

Then Haggai said, 'So it is with this people and this nation in my sight,' declares the Lord. 'Whatever they do and whatever they offer there is defiled.' (v. 14, NIV)

Did you resolve to eat more healthily at the beginning of January? Along with exercising and saving money, resolving to eat better is a top New Year's resolution. However, it is much easier to do this in community. If your family and friends hanker after takeaways or sugary treats and say to you, 'Go on, join us,' then you might find it hard to resist. However, when those close to you choose to eat a colourful array of vegetables, you might go for that nutritious choice as well. Good habits, and the opposite, can be catching, as we see in this passage.

We might wonder at God's change of tone here. After reading about God encouraging his people and promising that he won't leave them, why does he now focus on their sins and wrongdoing? In short, God doesn't want his people to lose an awareness of how destructive disobedience can be, and how quickly it can spread.

God reveals this truth through a series of questions about what is holy and what becomes defiled. Holiness cannot be 'caught', but defilement can. The warning is implied – to keep your hearts pure, keep them close to God.

Like choosing to enjoy a healthy array of food, staying close to God is much easier in community. When we're part of a church that loves the Bible, expresses devotion to God through spoken and sung worship, and reaches out to others in service, our faith will grow and flourish. Our church families can be a way of encountering God and being transformed by his love.

How's your relationship with church? If challenging, might God extend to you his love and healing, building up your hope? If encouraging, how can you notice and celebrate the riches you enjoy?

Loving God, I'm sorry for how I turn from you. Through your Holy Spirit, help me to stay committed to you. Nudge me throughout the day, that I may call on your presence with me to stay the course. Amen.

AMY BOUCHER PYE

Blessings ahead

'Give careful thought: is there yet any seed left in the barn? Until now, the vine and the fig-tree, the pomegranate and the olive tree have not borne fruit. From this day on I will bless you.' (vv. 18–19, NIV)

As I write this, we are preparing to move to southwest London after two decades in north London. I face the unknown with some fear and yet also hope for God's blessings in this new phase of life for our family. As I pray and ponder, I wonder if God is opening a path for us to flourish. That is, will he bless us in this?

I consider God's promises of blessings as I read of God speaking during the dedication of the foundation stone of the temple in this passage. This was an important community festival, steeped with meaning and significance. God chooses this moment to hearken his people to 'give careful thought' – repeating the phrase three times – before they lay the foundation stone. What past sins and acts of wrongdoing kept the wine vat from being full? What rot and mildew did their disobedience cause?

God wants them to pause and consider their past wrongdoing so that they don't repeat it in the present or the future. During this important public celebration, he cautions them to pause, to think carefully. As they do so, God then gives them hope for the future: 'From this day on I will bless you' (v. 19).

This moment of dedicating the second temple is a time to embrace God's promises to bless. So too can we notice and celebrate God's blessings during times of transition in our lives, even as we look back over our past actions, which may include disobedience. Whether we're moving to a new home and a new community, declaring our vows to love and honour a marriage partner, dedicating a baby to the Lord, or undertaking some other venture, we can hold on to God's promises that he won't leave us and that he will indeed bring blessings, not curses.

God, please help me to embody hope and faith when I have not yet embraced the new path in life that awaits me. I put my trust in you, believing your promises that you are faithful. Amen.

AMY BOUCHER PYE

Chosen one

'On that day,' declares the Lord Almighty, 'I will take you, my servant Zerubbabel son of Shealtiel,' declares the Lord, 'and I will make you like my signet ring, for I have chosen you,' declares the Lord Almighty. (v. 23, NIV)

As we wrap up our time in the book of Haggai, we land on this last section of God's message, which Haggai gave at the same time as our reading yesterday – during the dedication of the temple's foundation stone. In this passage God singles out Zerubbabel, the leader of God's people, with promises on a messianic level. God will, 'on that day', make him 'my servant' (v. 23), a name that God bestowed to Moses and David regularly. The 'on that day' would have been recognised by God's people as meaning 'the day of the Lord', the future times of God revealing himself fully to all nations. It's also interesting to note that Zerubbabel appears in the genealogy of Jesus in Matthew 1:12–13.

And the signet ring? This would be a precious possession of the chosen ones, signifying their status. They would take good care of it, wearing it with pride, as the Lord promises to do with Zerubbabel – and thus by extension all of his people. As they lay the foundation stone, God's message is one of hope, not only for that day but also for the future.

I hope and trust that our foray into this slim and often overlooked Old Testament book has strengthened your hope and faith in God. As he did centuries ago, God promises to be with us. We can continue to turn from our lives of sin through the work of his Holy Spirit with and within us. We need not fear, for God won't abandon us, and we can embrace his peace in all parts of our lives.

Whatever you're facing or experiencing, I pray that you will know not only with your head but also with your heart that God chooses you and delights in you.

Faithful and loving God, thank you for choosing me to be your beloved. Help me to fully embrace that status in all the moments of my life, that I might share your love and life with those I meet. Amen.

AMY BOUCHER PYE

Knowing God's love

Tracy Williamson writes...

When I was asked to write a series on this topic my heart leapt. To me, there is no greater theme than exploring God's love. Paul writes: 'I pray that you, being rooted and established in love, may have power, together with all the Lord's holy people, to grasp how wide and long and high and deep is the love of Christ, and to know this love that surpasses knowledge' (Ephesians 3:17–19, NIV).

God wants us to be rooted in his love and to discover just how big it is. However much we mess up, whatever our circumstances, guilt or brokenness, God never stops loving us. In these notes you will discover uplifting stories from both the Old and New Testaments of how God transformed peoples' lives with his love. You'll see his love offered in salvation and ministered in forgiveness and healing. You'll be uplifted by his comfort in times of loss and empowered to give his love away as you take on board that he's chosen you to be his channel.

None of this is just theory. My own childhood was marred by abuse, low self-esteem, fears and woundedness, and yet I can testify to the beautiful ways God has loved me, setting me free and empowering me to reach out to others. I pray these studies will encourage you to know that God's love is real and for you too. You are his beloved child, thought about with joy from the beginning of time. As his beloved, you'll discover his invitation to draw close, to listen for his voice and to experience that in his intimate knowing of you, you are completely safe. His knowing is the expression of his love for you, that he delights to sing over you and holds you close, rejoicing in your beauty. Safe in his love, you'll also find yourself challenged to let go of hard attitudes or to step out of your comfort zone.

Each note ends with a prayer, a challenge or a verse. These are for you to sit with quietly and absorb what God is showing you through that day's reading. Do engage with him in the confidence that he is with you, you are his treasure, and he longs to draw you deeper into that love that surpasses knowledge.

I hope you are blessed to read them as much as I have been blessed to write them.

For God so loved the world

For God so loved the world that he gave his one and only Son, that whoever believes in him shall not perish but have eternal life. For God did not send his Son into the world to condemn the world, but to save the world through him. (vv. 16–17, NIV)

If ever we long to see what's in God's heart and understand his ways, we have it here. Something had drawn Nicodemus to Jesus, and he had lots of questions. He wanted theological answers, but Jesus pointed him to the work of the Spirit. Nicodemus was relying on his logic, but Jesus emphasised that he needed to be born again.

It's important to bring our questions to Jesus, knowing that he delights to answer, but recognising that his answers will often surprise us. Nicodemus didn't understand, but he did keep asking. He was hungry for what he could see in Jesus, and Jesus honoured that. Jesus helped Nicodemus to understand that he could live as a new person, knowing God's loving presence within him, if only he believed.

John's follow-up comment, 'For God so loved the world', expresses the heart of what Jesus was telling Nicodemus. We need to know that God's ways are all rooted in his love. It is a love beyond imagining, as it encompasses the whole world. When I was growing up, I believed that everyone but me would be chosen and loved. I felt small and made any possibility of love for me small too, but John's words root the magnitude of God's love in his action. He gave us something priceless, the life of his own Son.

Like Nicodemus, I talked to Jesus one night when I had many questions and was desperate for answers. Some of those questions are still awaiting answers, but as I cried to him that night, something amazing happened. He came into my heart and started me on the journey of knowing his love. His love enlarges my thoughts and sets free my emotions. It is there for you and me, whatever the circumstances of our lives.

Father, thank you that you love me so much you let your only Son die for me. Lord, I believe. Please come into my heart. Help me to know you and grow in my heart knowledge of your love. Amen.

TRACY WILLIAMSON

When we feel crushed and under attack

I remember the days of long ago; I meditate on all your works and consider what your hands have done. I spread out my hands to you… Let the morning bring me word of your unfailing love, for I have put my trust in you. (vv. 5–6, 8, NIV)

Recently a friend reminded me of this lovely psalm. The context is that the enemy is attacking David, and he feels overwhelmed: 'He crushes me to the ground; he makes me dwell in the darkness like those long dead' (v. 3).

When we are in that dark place, God can seem far away, but he is committed to us and always gives us a way to overcome the devil's destructive lies. David responded to his situation by focusing on God's goodness and blessings. Similarly, we can either remember with sadness or with hope that what God did before he will do again.

I recently had sad news that made me feel very small. I wanted to hide and give up on everything, but friends encouraged me to remember ways that God had helped me before. David talks about considering God's ways, meditating on his works and spreading out our hands before him. This means giving God all the negative things and deliberately drinking in his love. There are always uplifting things we can listen to or read that will help us. Sharing with those who love us and will pray also strengthens us. In my situation, friends lifted me up and brought me God's comfort.

David said: 'Let the morning bring me word of your unfailing love' (v. 8). What we dwell on as we go to sleep is important. David expected that the morning would bring a special glimpse of God's love. With my bad news, my thoughts were in turmoil as I went to bed. I hardly prayed and was embracing hopelessness. I woke up feeling really ill. Since then, I've been trying to fix my heart on hope every night. That hope has been fulfilled as friends have reached out and prayed for me or I've seen something beautiful or uplifting.

God loves you with an everlasting love, and his mercies are new every morning. As you open your heart to his love, he will hold you in his everlasting arms, lift you up and enable you to soar.

TRACY WILLIAMSON

A father to the fatherless

A father to the fatherless, a defender of widows, is God in his holy dwelling. God sets the lonely in families, he leads out the prisoners with singing; but the rebellious live in a sun-scorched land. (vv. 5–6, NIV)

Amid all the powerful descriptions in Psalm 68 of God as majestic and unconquerable, these tender verses about him being a father to the fatherless stood out to me. I felt an ache of buried longing. My dad died when I was seven, and his place was soon filled by an abusive stepfather. I have experienced much healing from God, but the lack of any fatherly nurture or care in my life can still cause deep pain. This is a universal heart cry from many people who may look outwardly fine but inwardly are wounded.

Into the fissures of our global loss Father God is whispering words of healing love: 'I am your Father. I love you with an everlasting love. I see your fatherlessness, but I have come to restore you. From conception through to old age I am there to defend you, to protect and provide for you. I will not leave you orphaned. I come to you in tenderness to comfort your loneliness with words of love. Nothing can snatch you out of my hand.'

God has chosen us to be his children. As Father, he lovingly guides us into all his rich plans for us. He promises to always be there for us. When we make wrong choices, he gently convicts us, and when we repent, he takes our sin away and completely forgives us. He promises to meet all our needs, not necessarily by popping the solutions out like a chocolate bar from a vending machine, but so that we mature in our character and become rooted in his love.

I know God is healing my fatherlessness. God is committed to you as Father too. You are his beloved child. Let him touch all the places where you ache inside, and let them heal with his love.

Thank you, Father, that your love is so tender and that you say you delight in me. I want to be free to always live as your beloved child. May my enemies be scattered as I trust in you. Amen.

TRACY WILLIAMSON

Hearing we are loved

'If you remain in me and my words remain in you, ask whatever you wish, and it will be done for you. This is to my Father's glory, that you bear much fruit, showing yourselves to be my disciples. As the Father has loved me, so have I loved you.' (vv. 7–9, NIV)

Today, this passage in John 15 spoke to me of the importance of hearing God's word of love and choosing to root ourselves in its truth.

Jesus said: 'As the Father has loved me, so have I loved you. Now remain in my love' (v. 9).

Believing that I am loved has been a huge thing for me in my Christian journey, as I had so little experience of it as a child. Taking hold of that truth in faith has brought great healing over the years. Have you really taken in that you are loved in the same way that the Father loved Jesus? This is the foundation of your status as his beloved child. Jesus used the word 'remain' a lot. Remain means to live in it, think about it, bask and revel in it, and speak it out as a healing truth into inner areas of unbelief.

A disabled friend was praying. She felt low and said to the Lord: 'There are so many things I can't do.' He said: 'I love you.' She replied: 'But I can't walk and I'm awkward socially.' He said: 'I love you.' She'd always felt she couldn't hear him, and that was yet another factor in her low self-esteem. She realised that she was hearing God as he repeatedly said, 'I love you.' Soon after she started worshipping, expressively using her body in a way she had never felt free to do before. It's a wonderful witness to the power of God's love.

Jesus describes the power we'll be given as we open our hearts to his word. We'll be able to pray effectively and bear lasting fruit for him. Jesus said that this is to the Father's glory. I find it so wonderful that even in my weakness my life can glorify the Father's love.

Jesus says, 'I love you.' Have you heard him today? You can hear his voice. He wants to encourage you and show you beautiful things. Will you believe his words of love and bask in the joy of them?

TRACY WILLIAMSON

God hears our prayers

Then an angel of the Lord appeared to him, standing at the right side of the altar of incense. When Zechariah saw him, he was startled and was gripped with fear. But the angel said to him: 'Do not be afraid, Zechariah; your prayer has been heard.' (vv. 11–13, NIV)

I find this passage a real source of encouragement to pray with confidence in the knowledge that God loves us, and our prayers matter to him.

God breaks into Zechariah's routine to tell him that his prayers have been heard. Zechariah's response reveals that he'd given up praying long before. He and his wife Elizabeth were now old and could no longer have children. They'd settled for barrenness and buried their dreams, but God had always been planning to fulfil them, not just for their own sake but as part of his incredible plans. How awesome is God! It's so important that we trust God's love and his desire to answer our prayers. He can do more than we ask or imagine.

Are there things you have prayed about only to give up when it seems that God is ignoring you? Are you living a half-life, routinely doing your job or being part of church, but never expecting God to show up for you? God has no favourites. Just as he answered Zechariah's prayers at the right time, so he will answer your prayers too. Our faith is tested when we don't see an immediate answer, but we can be sure that our prayers touch God's heart and bring a shift in the heavenly realm.

I prayed for years that my mum would open her heart to the Lord before she died. In 2023 she went into an irreversible coma while in hospital. I sat by her bed, telling her repeatedly that God loved her. She showed no sign of hearing me and died the next morning at 9.00 am. Later I discovered that two friends had separately received visions from God at 9.00 am of my mum with Jesus, and I am sure he answered my prayers for her.

Lord Jesus, please forgive us when we give up praying. Fill our hearts with renewed faith and certain hope that our prayers matter and that through them you want to encourage us and do wonderful works to your glory. Amen.

TRACY WILLIAMSON

Sing, O daughter

Sing aloud, O daughter of Zion; shout, O Israel! Rejoice and exult with all your heart… The Lord your God is in your midst, a mighty one who will save; he will rejoice over you with gladness; he will quiet you by his love; he will exult over you with loud singing. (vv. 14, 17, ESV)

I have often struggled to grasp how deeply God loves me. As a child I always felt I was a disappointment and tried desperately to earn approval. Instead of the affirming words I longed for, there was constant mockery.

Maybe you've experienced similar hurt, and you are still carrying the scars today? In this passage, Zephaniah urges: 'Let not your hands grow weak' (v. 16). That's a good description of the emotional paralysis that can overwhelm us. But, as Zephaniah says, we can rejoice because God has taken away all judgement. Zephaniah's message is that God is always with his people and his desire is to lavish his love on us and bring freedom and rejoicing instead of fear.

The Lord gave me a picture as I read the words: 'He will rejoice over you with gladness.' I saw a young girl sitting alone and crying, her head buried in her arms. The Lord gathered her into his arms holding her close to his heart. He began to sing over her, the words expressing how beautiful she was, how much he delighted in her company and rejoiced to know what was on her heart. He was uninhibited in his love and, as he sang, she uncurled herself holding her head up high. The picture ended with them dancing together, a dance of intimacy and joy.

God wants to minister these truths to us all, especially those of us who feel crushed. Don't fear God's judgement, because Jesus has already carried it for you. God wants to quiet you by his love. He knows everything about your life and sees all your hidden acts of kindness that no one else sees. He rejoices over you and will never change his mind about you.

'I have deeply loved you with a forever-love; that is why I have been so patient and kind to draw you to my heart. You are precious to me, and I will build you up again' (Jeremiah 31:3–4, TPT).

TRACY WILLIAMSON

A woman transformed

Jesus said to her, 'You are right when you say you have no husband. The fact is, you have had five husbands, and the man you now have is not your husband. What you have just said is quite true.' 'Sir,' the woman said, 'I can see that you are a prophet.' (vv. 17–19, NIV)

This story is full of God's grace and transforming love. I love the way Jesus engaged this woman in conversation, while at the same time opening his heart to the promptings of the Holy Spirit. Jesus loves teaching us to tune into the Father's heart. So, as he sat quietly by the well, he was praying. Seeing the woman coming at midday, Jesus sensed her deep need and received wisdom as to how to gain her trust.

'Will you give me a drink?' he asked her. He wanted her to feel she could do something for him, that he valued her and what she could give, even though she was a Samaritan and her life was broken. God values you and me too. He sees deeper than our need, to the person he's created us to be. Jesus knew this woman was a thinker, and he wanted to stretch her theological understanding and show her that God loved her.

'Go, call your husband,' he said. I love the way he approached things so gently. Rather than fear, she became full of excitement. His love-infused knowledge transformed her and she started telling everyone in her village, 'Come, see a man who told me everything I've ever done'.

When I was suicidally depressed, a Christian student sensed God asking her to tell me that he loved me as a father. She didn't know that I'd lost my dad as a young child and my stepfather had abused me. Nor did she know that I'd tried to kill myself that very week. I was shocked at how spot on her words were. Like the Samaritan woman, God's words transformed me and can transform us all.

'Lord, you know everything there is to know about me… you understand my every thought before it even enters my mind… You read my heart like an open book' (Psalm 139:1–3, TPT).

TRACY WILLIAMSON

In times of sorrow

When Jesus saw her weeping, and the Jews who had come along with her also weeping, he was deeply moved in spirit and troubled. 'Where have you laid him?' he asked. 'Come and see, Lord,' they replied. Jesus wept. (vv. 33–35, NIV)

Are you feeling the pain of loss today? My heart is aching because of losing my lovely hearing dog Goldie and it being the anniversary of my mother's death.

How do we walk through loss? Some imply that it's wrong to mourn as it indicates a lack of faith, but the Bible teaches us that it's right to mourn even while we rejoice for the life lived. The psalms all express heartache as well as joy and hope.

In this story, we see how Jesus wept at Lazarus' tomb even though he knew that he would raise Lazarus to life. John tells us Jesus was deeply moved when he saw others grieving. Psalm 56:8 says: 'You have collected all my tears in your bottle' (NLT). In God's love for us he weeps, feeling our pain. He knows our sorrows and carried them to the cross. He came to be with us to bring comfort to all who mourn. Our tears matter, yet he alone can bring us real hope.

No one understood why Jesus didn't immediately rush to Lazarus. Like Mary and Martha, we too can feel disillusioned when we pray and nothing happens. I love how Jesus engaged with both sisters, patiently pointing them to the truth: 'I am the resurrection and the life' (v. 25).

As I prayed, I felt Jesus' assurance that my mother was safely with him. I miss her, but his word brings me great comfort. I know that Jesus is walking the 'darkest valley' with me, just as David expressed in Psalm 23. Companionship and understanding from a friend are so important, and Jesus is that friend always. He knows when we need to share, to have a hug, the kindness of a loving card or time out with a friend, and he will provide for those needs.

May you be filled with peace today, knowing that Jesus is with you. Underneath are his everlasting arms. If you are weeping, he weeps too, even while holding out to you his precious gift of comfort, hope and peace.

TRACY WILLIAMSON

Seeking his face

'Martha, Martha,' the Lord answered, 'you are worried and upset about many things, but few things are needed – or indeed only one. Mary has chosen what is better, and it will not be taken away from her.' (vv. 41–42, NIV)

Have you ever ranted about something only to find Jesus has a very different perspective? Knowing God's love means growing in self-awareness and making him our focus rather than cultural expectations.

Many of us, if we are honest, perhaps identify with Martha. She'd opened her home to Jesus and his friends. With no microwaves or freezers, food preparation was time-consuming, and Martha naturally expected her sister to share the work. After all, it was what women did! So, Martha's mini tirade when Mary sat at Jesus' feet rather than helping seems completely justified. Jesus, however, affirms Mary.

For Martha, nothing could be better than serving Jesus, but Jesus gently remonstrates with her: 'You are worried and upset about many things.' He acknowledges her feelings, but he was looking deeper and seeing into the hidden things that drove her. Jesus wanted to set her free.

Do we let Jesus shine his light on our hidden attitudes? It can be scary, but his insights are full of transforming wisdom. Jesus wants our heart love and always calls us to make listening to him our highest goal.

Mary knew that even if it shocked people, she needed to sit with Jesus and drink in his words. This same Mary later used her hair to dry Jesus' feet as she wept in gratitude. Could it be that it was on this occasion that she suddenly understood the depth of Jesus' forgiveness and opened her heart to receive? I'm sure Martha's heart was also changed as she heard Jesus' gentle rebuke. Jesus' words are always life-changing. He loves us unconditionally and will always seek to free us and draw us deeper into his love. Will we seek his face?

Forgive me, Lord, for every way I'm driven by cultural drives and expectations. Thank you for your amazing love for me. Your words are full of power and loving insight. Set me free to love you above all else. Amen.

TRACY WILLIAMSON

The empowering treasure

Peter said, 'Silver or gold I do not have, but what I do have I give you. In the name of Jesus Christ of Nazareth, walk.' Taking him by the right hand, he helped him up, and instantly the man's feet and ankles became strong. He jumped to his feet and began to walk. (vv. 6–8, NIV)

The Lord loves to use us, and the more we know his love, the greater the transformation and hope we can bring to those around us.

This story is not just about a healing miracle, but the power of a heart healed by Jesus. Peter has found an incredible treasure: the knowledge that Jesus has forgiven him and embraces him despite his weaknesses. Even though Peter failed in the past, Jesus is using him to minister to this broken man and to feed his sheep. It's as if Peter has moved from the shade to the sunshine, and everything is different.

Instead of his old impetuous reactions, we see spiritual maturity in Peter's response as the man accosts him. 'Peter looked straight at him', and then said to the man: 'Look at us!' (v. 4). In that short pause, Peter made an inner choice to listen for what the Holy Spirit shows him of Jesus' heart. Out of that choice came the certainty – 'Silver or gold I do not have, but what I do have I give you' (v. 6) – and the resulting miracle.

Do you know what you have? Are you nurturing and growing in God's love for you and seeing it as a source of inner power? Have you allowed him to heal that hurting place deep inside?

I am always so aware of my weaknesses. I can make my deafness or my childhood struggles an impassable mountain, but as I've received God's healing love and then reached out to others, I've seen Jesus use those very things to touch people's lives with his comfort and peace.

Jesus calls us 'beloved' and gives us the treasure of his love, forgiveness and constant presence. Let's be ready to pause, just as Peter did, recognise afresh what we have and then give it away.

Lord Jesus, please heal my brokenness and help me, like Peter, to always be ready to listen to you and to live from the centre of your love. May others know your healing as I reach out in your name. Amen.

TRACY WILLIAMSON

God's surprising grace

Then the word of the Lord came to him: 'Go at once to Zarephath in the region of Sidon and stay there. I have instructed a widow there to supply you with food.' So he went to Zarephath. (vv. 8–10, NIV)

I've been reflecting on this story of the widow of Zarephath and how it illustrates God's surprising grace and care for the tiniest details of our lives.

The story opens with famine because of the lack of rain prophesied by Elijah. God had led Elijah to a certain brook, but it had suddenly dried up. We all hit those times of barrenness. Maybe you've seen wonderful answers to prayer and known the joy of worship, but now your prayers feel empty and your joy has disappeared. Is that you today?

Elijah desperately needed to find water and food, and God told him to go to Zarephath, as he had directed a widow there to supply him. Why would God use a widow from a foreign nation to provide for his prophet? It doesn't make sense, especially as she was starving. Why not use someone who was wealthy enough to source their water and food? However, as she obeyed God's call to feed Elijah, even before she fed herself, God miraculously provided for her, her son and Elijah throughout the remainder of the famine.

God loves to use us whatever our circumstances, and he knows every detail of our lives, as we see when Elijah arrives at the town gate to find the widow there gathering sticks. What incredible timing! God knows when we sit or stand. Psalm 139:3 says that he is intimately acquainted with all our ways. His love for us is bigger than we can ever imagine.

God cared for that widow as deeply as he cared for Elijah. He wanted to do a miracle beyond providing for her own and Elijah's needs, to reveal his glory through her into that godless region. Like her, we are all chosen to be part of his amazing plans of redemption and love.

God's plans are always much bigger than ours, but he uses us in amazing ways to fulfil them. May you experience his surprising grace today to meet your needs and make his glory known to those around you.

TRACY WILLIAMSON

Chosen for this moment

'The king has but one law: that they be put to death unless the king extends his gold sceptre to them...' [Mordecai] sent back this answer:... 'Who knows but that you have come to your royal position for such a time as this?' (vv. 11, 13, 14, NIV)

While knowing God's love includes experiencing his nurture, affirmation and care, he also calls us to be ambassadors of his love. Sometimes that involves stepping out to do things that terrify us.

Satan lies to us that we are inferior and uses fear to keep us from rising up in our God-given authority. Fear was Esther's immediate response when Mordecai asked her to go to the king to plead for the Jews. In that moment, the fear of death was all Esther could focus on. She was distressed for her people, but she was bound by her fear. How often do we react to difficult challenges like that?

My tough early life robbed me of self-esteem, and even now I often feel paralysed by fear. When my mum needed help with personal care, I wanted to run away. What might go wrong seemed much more of a certainty than a divine miracle. However, as I stepped out in love, I saw God at work. In the months before my mum died, I was able to help her in very personal ways, and I do believe a door opened in her heart to the Lord's love and that she is with him now.

When Mordecai challenged Esther, 'Who knows but that you have come to your royal position for such a time as this?' (v. 14), something shifted. She suddenly knew that she was indeed chosen, and God's love empowered her to act, despite knowing she might be killed. As a result, the Jews were saved from a terrible genocide.

We too are chosen by God. We are his royal representatives 'for such a time as this'. We will have incredible impact on our world as we pray and act out of God's love and anointing rather than hiding away in fear.

Father, thank you that you have given me royal authority. Help me not to focus on negatives but to rise up and, through my prayers and actions, bring divine transformation to the situations I face. In Jesus' name. Amen.

TRACY WILLIAMSON

Constantly with us

For He has said, 'I will never [under any circumstances] desert you [nor give you up nor leave you without support, nor will I in any degree leave you helpless], nor will I forsake or let you down or relax My hold on you [assuredly not]!' (v. 5, AMP)

I'm always encouraged by God's promise to be with us. He promised it to many fearful people in the Old Testament, to give them courage and strength.

Jesus declared before his ascension: 'I am with you always, to the very end of the age' (Matthew 28:20, NIV). He promises to be with us always. There is never a moment when he is not alongside us. He is with me now as I sit at my computer, and he is with you too.

Today's reading in Hebrews reminds us of the importance of living our lives in the knowledge that God is constantly with us. Our thoughts and actions should all flow out of the knowledge of his loving presence. In verse 5 the writer quotes God's reassurance to Joshua: 'I will never leave you nor forsake you' (Joshua 1:5, NIV). As I read, I found myself praying: 'Lord, what does that look like in practice?' I sensed him saying that he wanted to open my eyes to heavenly understanding, even in the midst of my everyday activities. I was about to fry some eggs and thought, 'Well, there's not many insights you can give me through this job, Lord.'

God loves to surprise us. I sensed him encouraging me to watch the eggs and have eyes to perceive. I broke them into the pan, and in seconds the slippery, transparent white took substance. The thought came: 'Never be afraid of times of heat or even fire. I am with you, working to shape and form you, to give you substance and depth. I have given you the treasure of my presence and love, but sometimes it's going through the fire that makes my life within you become real and visible. Don't be afraid. I love you. Rather than fighting those times, treasure them, for they will birth beautiful treasure in you.'

I pray you will experience God opening your eyes and ears through the ordinary things that make up your day, and that you too will experience great joy as you receive his insights.

TRACY WILLIAMSON

Prayer – language of love and power

'Do not store up for yourselves treasures on earth, where moths and vermin destroy, and where thieves break in and steal. But store up for yourselves treasures in heaven… For where your treasure is, there your heart will be also.' (vv. 19–21, NIV)

A friend was saying how vital quality communication is with those we love. The Lord spoke through her words, communicating his longing for me to enjoy talking with him just as I do with my friends.

Sometimes my prayers feel like a ritual, something I have to do as a Christian, but I know that God loves to encourage and heal us as we pray. He also uses us as channels of his love, power and authority against the enemy. I'm discovering afresh just what a privilege prayer is as it enables me to know God's heart and partner with him in his plans.

Jesus said, 'Store up for yourselves treasure in heaven' (v. 20). Receiving God's love and hearing his voice are irreplaceable treasures. The first time I heard him, he said he wanted to be a father to me. I was in deep distress, but that word started me on a healing journey, and out of it I've helped many others.

So, how can we pray? Jesus taught his disciples to pray: 'Our Father in heaven' (v. 9). The starting point of Jesus' prayer guide is our relationship with our Father God. Do you know that your heavenly Father loves to spend time with you? Your needs matter to him. He loves you with an unchanging love. Build this into your heart and prayer can become a love encounter between father and beloved child. He told me once as I gazed at a beautiful landscape that I was even more beautiful! I was stunned because I'd always been told I was ugly. This word brought me great healing.

With 'hallowed be your name' (v. 9), Jesus teaches us to declare God's goodness and love rather than the negatives. As we dwell in God's desire to bless us, something amazing happens in the spiritual realm, defeating Satan's lies and releasing God's will on earth.

Spend a while at the start of your prayer times drinking in God's incredible love. Your prayers will take on a new dimension of joy and certainty, out of which will flow the power to do his wonderful works.

TRACY WILLIAMSON

About time

Lyndall Bywater writes…

I recently discovered that I possess an unusual gift. I always know, to within 15 or 20 minutes, what time it is. This is true even when I'm not wearing a watch and haven't checked the time for hours. The only exception is when I wake up from being asleep. I used to think everyone could do this, but apparently not.

It's a mixed blessing, to be honest. I love the sense of knowing where I am in relation to the hours of the day, but I also always feel bound to the passage of time in some way – rarely able to just switch off and enjoy the now.

This series is all about time, and it's given me a fascinating opportunity to look more deeply into how God sees time and the various ways in which we interact with it. We will be considering the way God formed our world to operate in cycles and seasons, and we will be reflecting on how God then chooses to operate outside of these rules when the need arises. We'll be exploring what it means to entrust our times to God, thinking about Jesus and his promise that 'the time has come', and we will be pondering some of the things Paul has to say about time too. We'll also be looking at how time can help to bring forth healing and justice.

In truth, this set of Bible notes has given me an interesting challenge, because it turns out that talking about time is much like talking about the air we breathe or the substance we're made of. Time is such an intrinsic part of our existence that it can be hard to get enough distance from it to have a good look at it. Over the next two weeks, we will look at some of the most famous scriptures about time, and we will ponder together how we might live more fully into every moment.

I hope and pray that these readings will encourage you, challenge you, and set you thinking about things you may not often give much thought to. I hope and pray you will discover more about the wonders of God's creation and even more about the limitless love which God has for you.

A fitting rhythm

Then God said, 'Let lights appear in the sky to separate the day from the night. Let them be signs to mark the seasons, days, and years. Let these lights in the sky shine down on the earth.' And that is what happened. (vv. 14–15, NLT)

How's your circadian rhythm? That's the rhythm which your body follows so it knows when to wake up and when to sleep. If your circadian rhythm is disrupted, as it often is for shift workers, for example, your brain doesn't know which messages to send to your body at what time of day, and that disruption can be debilitating, affecting your sleep, eating patterns and even your mental health.

The circadian rhythm is one of the most amazing facets of creation. It was the God of the universe who gave us this planet to be our home, perfectly positioned to sustain our life, and who made for us a rhythm of hours, a sacred rotation of waking and sleeping, eating and fasting, working and resting. We are designed to operate within that rhythm, because it fits us and we fit it.

In our desire to get things done, it's all too easy to let ourselves become so busy that we stretch this fragile rhythm out of shape by overfilling our days. However, we can't survive like that for long. Eventually the rhythm catches up with us and we realise we are going to need to respect the boundaries and limitations which God's gracious 24-hour cycle sets for us.

As one who's rather prone to stuffing too much into my life, I have developed the habit of picturing the day ahead as a basket, handed to me by God, into which I can fit a certain number of things. It's important that it's a basket: beautifully woven and sturdy enough, but not limitless and not able to contain vast quantities without breaking. I then reflect on what will fit well into that basket; what can I fit into my day without bursting the seams of this precious rhythm God has given me?

Imagine today as that beautifully woven basket, totally different from yesterday or tomorrow. What has God put in it for you? What will you put in it yourself? What do you need to leave out, so it doesn't get too full?

LYNDALL BYWATER

A fruitful rotation

For everything there is a season, a time for every activity under heaven. A time to be born and a time to die. A time to plant and a time to harvest... Yet God has made everything beautiful for its own time. He has planted eternity in the human heart, but even so, people cannot see the whole scope of God's work from beginning to end. (vv. 1–2, 11, NLT)

I do love a good gardening show on the radio or TV, but I confess I have yet to turn any of my enthusiastically acquired theory into practice, mainly because I live with someone who is a very talented gardener already. The part of gardening shows that always fascinates me is when they talk about what you can do in the garden at the different times of the year. I love the idea that there is always a job to do, even when everything seems to be asleep or dead.

Yesterday we thought about the precious gift of days. Today we reflect on the precious gift of seasons. These are perhaps the most famous verses in Ecclesiastes, and they remind us of the truth that our planet is designed to turn through a cycle of life and death, growth and decay. In a world where we can buy pretty much any fruit and vegetable at any time of year, these are important things to be reminded of, not least because those cycles of life and death are an outward sign of the inner realities of our own lives.

As gardening programmes have taught me, there are certain things which can only be done in certain seasons of the year, and the same is true in us. The work God is doing in our lives is right for the season we're in. We may wish it could be different. We may wish for the spiritual or emotional equivalent of Kentish strawberries in January, but in the end we do well to recognise and embrace the season we're in. Our God is a gardener who sees the full scope of our lives from beginning to end and knows how to bring forth fruit in us at the right time.

Spend some time looking through the 'a time to...' phrases in this passage from Ecclesiastes. Which catches your attention? Are there any which seem to fit the season you're in at the moment?

LYNDALL BYWATER

It's all relative

For you, a thousand years are as a passing day, as brief as a few night hours... Teach us to realise the brevity of life, so that we may grow in wisdom. (vv. 4, 12, NLT)

If you found a dark enough place and the conditions were right, you might just be able to see the planet Uranus without a telescope. You might be astounded to know that it's just under two billion miles from Earth. The light you would be seeing reflected from its surface would have taken over two and a half hours to reach your eyes. If you then found yourself a telescope, you could start looking at objects in the night sky which are so far away that their light takes years and years to reach us.

I'm no scientist, and these figures blur my brain when I think of them, but they also help me to remember that, just as this little planet of ours with its rhythms and seasons is part of something so much bigger, so our little lives are held in the hands of a God who is far more vast than I could ever comprehend. The writer of Psalm 90 seems to have been pondering the same idea too, that God operates on an entirely different scale to us humans. While we count in days, God counts in millennia; while we mark the seasons, God watches whole lifetimes come and go.

Talk of millennia and distant planets might seem daunting, but the psalmist found it helped him to get perspective on the brevity and fragility of his own life. We get so caught up in the minute details of our little days, but maybe it would help, every so often, if we remember that the one who created us holds entire galaxies together, so our very human problems really aren't a problem to God.

Next time you panic that things won't get done in time, remind yourself that your almighty creator God has all time and eternity to hand.

If you want to get your life into perspective but don't fancy stargazing, find a big old tree to sit under. Examine its trunk and its branches and reflect on how many generations it has seen come and go.

LYNDALL BYWATER

It's all in hand

My times are in your hand; deliver me from the hand of my enemies and persecutors. (v. 15, NRSV)

I'm sitting down to write this daily Bible note in the knowledge that I have an hour before I need to go out. So, I can promise you with absolute certainty that the next 60 minutes will fly by, partly because I'm having fun, of course, but also because time always seems to fly when there's a deadline to meet. On the other hand, next time I'm doing something I don't enjoy at all, you can bet it will feel like time has slowed almost to a stop. Our reading yesterday talked about how a thousand years are like a day to God, and I've certainly lived through a few days that felt like a thousand years.

The psalmist who wrote Psalm 31 is in a difficult situation. Life has become one long round of battles and betrayal, grief and rejection. I imagine it must have felt like time was moving very slowly indeed. Having poured out his heart to God about how out of control he feels, he suddenly reaches for a key truth. He reminds himself that his times are in God's hand.

It is this shift of perspective which helps us weather the tough stuff: the truth that, no matter how slowly or quickly, how well or badly our times seem to be going, they are always and forever in the hands of the God who loves us. When we feel like we're in the hand of the enemy, like our destiny is at the mercy of those who want to harm us, there's courage in the truth that we and our times are held in the hand of the one who is the beginning and the end, who calls time on the enemy's schemes, and who rescues us in the nick of time.

Are you in a situation where it feels like time is going too slowly or too quickly? Remind yourself that God holds your life. You might even like to picture it there, cupped in the strong, warm hand of God.

LYNDALL BYWATER

Tinkering with time

And the sun stood still, and the moon stopped until the nation took vengeance on their enemies. Is this not written in the Book of Jashar? The sun stopped in midheaven and did not hurry to set for about a whole day. (Joshua 10:13, NRSV)

Escape Rooms have become very popular over recent years. If you're not familiar with the concept, it basically involves a group of people being locked in a room (whether physical or virtual) and having to solve a series of puzzles within a certain time period to 'escape'. While the puzzles can be tricky in themselves, the real challenge is the time limit, and the experience plays on the stress we feel when we're up against the clock. After all, time waits for no one… or does it?

God created our world to turn in days and seasons, initiating the stream of time which flows constantly and relentlessly towards its ending, and humanity is held within that steady stream. Yet the two stories in today's passages tell of moments when God interrupted that stream, making time stand still or even pushing it backwards. Two powerful men needed a sign from God, something to show them (and those around them) that there is a God who stands above and outside of the created order, and God chose to do that by stretching time itself.

I love the idea that Father God sometimes breaks the rules of his own created order just to show us more of who he is. Being a person with poor time management, I have often prayed that God would stop time for me so I can catch a train or meet a deadline. God usually tells me to live with the consequences and get better at planning my diary, but just occasionally I have known God to stretch the time available so that I can fit a supernatural number of things into it. It's an amazing experience which always leaves me in awe of the God who made time itself, and for whom nothing is impossible.

Do you ever pray over the time you have available? If time feels too short or too tight, why not ask God to help you, either by showing you how to fit everything in or by stretching time for you?

LYNDALL BYWATER

Accelerating time

'He changes times and seasons; he deposes kings and raises up others. He gives wisdom to the wise and knowledge to the discerning.' (v. 21, NIV)

On 8 December 2024, President Bashar al-Assad of Syria was deposed. His almost 25-year rule had been a cruel dictatorship, quick to use violence to suppress any opposition, and only time will tell the story of the human rights violations which took place on his watch. His downfall was remarkably swift in the end. Rebel forces took less than two weeks to overthrow his regime and send him into exile.

Today's passage gives us a chance to eavesdrop on a conversation between a prophet and a dictator. Nebuchadnezzar ruled by suppression and domination, and he had a formidable reputation for eliminating his enemies. With no democratic process to limit his time in office, those under his rule might reasonably have feared living for years and years at his mercy. Daniel has come to interpret Nebuchadnezzar's dream, and that dream turns out to be a sober warning; the God who created time itself is also the God who can change times and seasons at will. Nebuchadnezzar may have great power, but the one who is enthroned above all powers can break off his rule in an instant. Our loving Father is not a distant observer watching history play out. He is sovereign, and the empires of the earth rise and fall at his behest.

We will never know how many prayers were prayed in Syria, believers crying out to God to change the times and seasons and to bring in a new era, but the speed of the liberation suggests God's miraculous power was at work. When time seems to be stuck in an endless loop of oppression and tyranny, it's heartening to know that God can break the iron grip of the most powerful ruler overnight, and it's an encouragement to us to keep praying for those situations where change seems impossible.

Take some time to pray for Syria today, that God will help the Syrian people to walk into real and complete freedom, and that the church will shine the light of the good news of Jesus brightly across the land.

LYNDALL BYWATER

Knowing the times

Day after day men came to help David, until he had a great army, like the army of God. These are the numbers of the men armed for battle who came to David... from Issachar, men who understood the times and knew what Israel should do – 200 chiefs, with all their relatives under their command. (vv. 22–23, 32, NIV)

Whether it's telling a joke, baking a cake or landing a plane, it's true what they say: timing is everything. It's one thing to know how to do something – to have the skills required to undertake a task – but it's another thing entirely to know when to act. That often involves a layer of wisdom which only comes with a lot of experience.

David needed an army, and fortunately his popularity was on the rise. Men from the various tribes of Israel came to support him, bringing their particular gifts. Some were highly experienced militia armies; some had impressive arrays of weaponry; some were less numerous and less well-equipped but brought heart and courage. And then there were the men of Issachar, the only ones who didn't rate a mention for their military prowess at all. They brought a very different gift: the gift of understanding the times.

These men were described as 'chiefs', which suggests they were wise elders and seasoned leaders. They were probably skilled observers of the ways of humankind and would have had a good grasp of Israel's history. But they were also prophets. We're told they knew what Israel should do, which suggests they had cultivated deep, God-given insight. We sometimes think that people are either the cerebral type (researching and analysing) or the Spirit-led type (spontaneous and feelings-orientated), but that's a false dichotomy. If we truly want to know the times, we need to be committed to both aspects of the Issachar gifting. We need to study and observe to deepen our understanding of the world we live in, and we need to give time to prayer and spiritual practices to help us open our spiritual eyes and ears to sense where God is moving.

Have you had any 'Issachar people' in your life – people who have helped you understand what time you're in and what course of action you should take? Why not make time today to write and thank them for their wisdom.

LYNDALL BYWATER

God's time

'The least of you will become a thousand, the smallest a mighty nation. I am the Lord; in its time I will do this swiftly.' (v. 22, NIV)

We'd been discussing moving house for ages, but nothing had quite fallen into place. Then one day we found the property which we were fairly certain was right for us, so we booked a viewing. When we arrived, the estate agent informed us that we couldn't go in because she couldn't get the key to work. Could we come back another day? It was the logical thing to do, but something in me resisted. I just had a feeling this was the time, so I asked if we could try the key ourselves. We did, and with a bit of wiggling and a lot of prayer, the door opened.

This chapter of Isaiah is full of promises about destiny, restoration and fulfilment – huge things for which we might pray about for years without ever seeing results – but then it finishes with a verse which, for me at least, is a bit of a lightbulb moment. It finishes with the promise that these things will happen swiftly, but only when it's God's time.

It's easy to think that the waiting and unanswered prayers are something to do with the fact that we haven't quite got it right yet, but often I suspect it's more about needing to wait for God's perfect timing. I can easily think it'd be more convenient if God could send me a signal – perhaps an alert on my phone – to let me know when that perfect time has arrived, so I can skip all the frustration and disappointment, but in truth I know that those seasons of prayerful waiting help to prepare me for whatever God wants to give me.

We moved into our new house just three months after that first viewing. When God's time does arrive, the fulfilment of the promise often comes swiftly.

It may not be God's time for the thing we long for most, but it's always God's time for something. Why not take a moment in prayer to ask: 'Lord, what is it your time for in my life today?'

LYNDALL BYWATER

The time has come

After John was put in prison, Jesus went into Galilee, proclaiming the good news of God. 'The time has come,' he said. 'The kingdom of God has come near. Repent and believe the good news!' (vv. 14–15, NIV)

There are so many different types of waiting, aren't there? There's the patient, slightly bored waiting you do when you're queueing or waiting for a train on a cold platform, and then there's the irrepressible, bubbling over kind of waiting which happens when you are about to do something thrilling.

These different kinds of waiting go with the different kinds of time which the Bible talks about. So far, we've focused mainly on *chronos* time – the passing of days and seasons, the stream of time which God has set in motion and which God has charge over. When you're waiting in a queue or longing for the train to arrive, you're attending the passing of *chronos*. Today we move to *kairos* time, a moment of significance... the kind of moment that you wait for with breathless excitement.

We read yesterday in Isaiah that when God's time arrives, the fulfilment will happen swiftly. Well, here we are. Jesus chooses to begin his ministry by telling his followers that God's time has come! The moment has arrived, and that kingdom, so beautifully depicted in Isaiah, is near. The atmosphere must have been electric because four fishermen got so excited that they immediately left their livelihoods and followed this little-known Galilean.

That *kairos* moment was 2,000 years ago, but one of the things about *kairos* moments is that they sit outside of *chronos* time. Jesus' invitation to seize this God-moment and to get involved in this glorious kingdom which is coming near is as live and thrilling today as it was 2,000 years ago, and it is meant for us!

The time is now. Lord, forgive us when these words become so familiar that we lose the wonder of them. Fill us with the same excitement that caused those fishermen to abandon everything and follow you. Amen.

LYNDALL BYWATER

Now time

For God says, 'At just the right time, I heard you. On the day of salvation, I helped you.' Indeed, the 'right time' is now. Today is the day of salvation. (2 Corinthians 6:2, NLT)

Speaker and author Joyce Meyer once said: 'Patience is not simply the ability to wait, it's how we behave while we're waiting.'

When I read those words, I think of the story of Simeon and Anna, two people who had spent decades waiting for the Messiah. You could argue that all Jewish believers were waiting for the Messiah, but Simeon and Anna hadn't just pushed the idea to the back of their minds and got on with other things; they had waited actively, going to the temple and seeking him out. They had taken the trouble to understand the times in which they lived and the promises of God in scripture, and now they were standing in front of the answer to all their hopes and dreams.

I can't help wondering what they did next. What did they do with this astonishing realisation that salvation was no longer a future hope but a present reality. I imagine they told all sorts of people what they'd seen, but did they also change the way they prayed? Did they expect to see new and wonderful things they'd never seen before?

We are all too familiar with the news that the Messiah has come, and it's easy to take that knowledge for granted. Do we perhaps need a bit of Simeon and Anna's delight or the excitement Paul felt when he quoted to the Corinthians the Old Testament scripture about this being the right time and the day of salvation being 'now'? Of course, that doesn't mean we get everything we want or that our prayers get answered instantaneously, but it does mean that we live in the constant joy of knowing that the wellspring of love, wholeness, deliverance, healing and peace is open and flowing, right here, right now.

What difference will it make to your life today to know that today is the day of salvation? What will you ask for? What will you expect? What will you risk? What will you get excited about?

LYNDALL BYWATER

The fullness of time!

But when the fullness of time had come, God sent his Son, born of a woman, born under the law, in order to redeem those who were under the law, so that we might receive adoption as children. (vv. 4–5, NRSV)

Are you an ahead-of-time person or a behind-time person? You'll know the answer to this when I ask you whether you tend to put something down before you've finished it in order to make a prompt start on the next thing in your to-do list, or whether you find it hard to stop what you're doing before you've finished it, so you tend to keep going till the last moment and then end up being late to the next thing. I'm definitely the latter, and consequently I am overfamiliar with the sound of people shouting: 'Lyndall, it's time to go!'

Yesterday we were reminding ourselves that Jesus has arrived. We're now in this *kairos* moment, when the things of God's kingdom are supposed to be happening all around us. But in today's passage we find Paul frustrated with new believers who seem to be living by an old pattern.

Paul uses a beautiful phrase to describe this new kingdom era. He says that the fullness of time has come – as though something has been brewing, stirring, building, and suddenly it's ready. Suddenly we've ticked over into a totally different time, and he's adamant that the Galatians should be living in this era, not the old one. These aren't even Jewish believers he's talking to, but still they seem to have found a kind of enslavement to law, which they were calling Christianity.

It's important to ask ourselves: have we got stuck in old patterns? Are we really enjoying the life and freedom won for us in this new kingdom era or are we still living out an Old Testament sort of slavery to rules and rituals? Are we ready to move on? Is the Spirit shouting at us to tell us it's time to go?

Holy Spirit, show me where I am living in old patterns, governed by rules that aren't from you, missing out on the wonder of kingdom nearness. Breathe on me again, and bring me to life in this glorious new era. Amen.

LYNDALL BYWATER

Time grows

So let's not get tired of doing what is good. At just the right time we will reap a harvest of blessing if we don't give up. (v. 9, NLT)

I was sitting in a train station scrolling through social media, mostly because I'd just received some truly sad news and I wasn't enjoying the company of my own thoughts, when I came across a post about grief. The writer explained that, in her experience, it isn't so much that our grief gets smaller or less important over time; it's that time allows us to build up the muscles we need to carry our grief. That revelation proved a great blessing to me in the days to come.

In today's passage, Paul is considering the idea of time in relation to planting, tending and harvesting. It's a metaphor he comes back to often, encouraging the believers in those fledgling churches to keep cultivating their faith, even when things seem too hard. Perhaps he likes the image of gardening because it emphasises our partnership with God. We do the planting and the watering, but only God can do the growing. And because God does the growing, God gets to determine exactly the right moment for the harvest.

Maybe you're carrying pain or grief at the moment and someone has told you that time heals. I'm not sure about that, but I do know that God heals. I also know that God uses time to grow things, especially when we join in by 'doing what is good', as Paul puts it. When it comes to grief, doing good means things like expressing your feelings, talking to trusted friends and skilled professionals, and pouring out your heart to God in prayer. When you do that, God will grow muscles in your soul, muscles that will help you to carry the experiences life has brought. Then, when that growing is done, at just the right time, you will harvest the healing you so long for.

Have you seen any of your friends or family journeying through grief? How have they changed or grown through the process? What muscles did you see God grow in them? Pray that they will know God's comfort today.

LYNDALL BYWATER

Give it time

'Let both of them grow together until the harvest, and at harvest time I will tell the reapers, Collect the weeds first and bind them in bundles to be burned, but gather the wheat into my barn… The Son of Man will send his angels, and they will collect out of his kingdom all causes of sin and all evildoers.' (vv. 30, 41, NRSV)

I was about three when I learnt the word 'antagonise'. I wasn't a child prodigy or anything, it's just that me and my big brother were so good at winding each other up that our parents were forever telling us to stop antagonising each other. Like most siblings, we enjoyed irritating each other, but hated it when the other one returned the favour. If we felt we'd been treated unjustly in any way, we would bemoan the unfairness and demand that our parents put things right immediately, punishing the guilty party and proving us right. Children rarely have any concept of delayed justice, and we were no exception.

In today's passage, Jesus tells a parable of a flagrant injustice. A farmer has an enemy who has deliberately contaminated his crop with weeds. On the face of it, surely the right thing to do would be to rectify the situation as soon as possible, yet that's not what the farmer chooses. His wealth of experience means he knows his crop, and he also knows the species of weed that has been sown. His expertise tells him that he will get a better crop if he gives his field time, letting the wheat get stronger and letting the weeds mature so that they're easier to distinguish at harvest time.

When an injustice has been done, it can be hard to let things take their course. Lack of resolution feels like letting evil get away with it or like God doesn't care, but time is a powerful revealer. It can bring truth to light. It can bring forth the good in the worst of situations. It can 'ripen' a situation to the point where we can reap a much fuller justice than the justice we'd have got if we'd acted instantly.

This parable isn't a licence to ignore injustice. We may need to give time for situations to take their course, but how can we tend the wheat? How can we lend support to the people involved who may be suffering?

LYNDALL BYWATER

The end of time

And the city has no need of sun or moon to shine on it, for the glory of God is its light, and its lamp is the Lamb. (v. 23, NRSV)

I was having a conversation with a friend of mine about the book of Revelation once, and he suddenly said, in a thoroughly disgruntled voice: 'So basically God's going to blow up all the stuff I really love – rivers, mountains, trees, animals, stars – and all we're going to be left with is endless singing!' I enjoy a good sing as much as the next person, but I could see his point. When we read Revelation and try to approximate it to something we have experience of, the closest we can get is that it's going to be one long church service with some strange creatures in the mix.

One of the reasons that sounds so unbearable is because we have forgotten to remove the concept of time from our imaginings. When we think about doing something endlessly, we're thinking about an ever-longer stretch of time, and when you do the same thing for a long time, it becomes boring. In today's passage, we read that there will be no more sun or moon. I don't think that's about whether there will be stars and planets in the new creation. I think it is the writer's way of conveying that the cycle of days, inaugurated by God in Genesis, will end. No longer will we mark off our time in chunks of past, present and future. The stream of *chronos* time will be no more; we will live in one vast, beautiful, joyful *kairos* moment (and the singing will be optional)!

Time is a precious gift, but it also has limitations: endings and partings, rushing for deadlines and battling busyness. Time is a line along which we can only fit so much, but eternity is the wide-open space where everything fits, everything comes together, and everything is now.

Loving God, you guide us through the stream of time towards your eternity. Reassure us when time flies too fast, and inspire us when it runs slow. Teach us to make the most of every precious moment you give us. Amen.

LYNDALL BYWATER

Isaiah 43

Amy Boucher Pye writes…

Lovely friend, how glad I am that we get to spend a week together with a favourite scripture passage, Isaiah 43 (and a few verses from the next chapter). As we move into a new month, I trust that you'll feel affirmed and inspired by the ancient words of this Old Testament prophet, which pulse with life today.

In my 20s, in a time of a great need, I found God speaking to me lovingly through the Bible. As I personalised various passages, dropping my name into the text as a way of embracing the truths with my head and my heart, I found the words of Isaiah 43 riveting. 'Don't be afraid, Amy, for I've saved you…' I wrote in my journal. 'You're passing through the waters, but don't be afraid, for I'm with you.' I felt God's love wrap around me snugly, comforting me. Then I arrived at verse 4: 'You're precious and honoured in my sight.' I wondered if its words were really true. *Lord, do you really love me? Is this promise meant for me?* I paused and felt a resounding *Yes* in my spirit. I thought, *Well, I could be wrong, but it's right here in the Bible, so maybe God really does mean this…*

God continued to speak to me through the Bible in that early flowering of my faith, and he still brings the scriptures alive for me today. I trust he'll never stop speaking to me, and I believe he speaks to you too.

This week we'll be looking at six themes from this passage, and I'll give background and context about the situation Isaiah lived in, about which God was so concerned. Our six themes are:

1 Fear not, I've redeemed you (Isaiah 43:1)
2 You're my witnesses (v. 10)
3 I am the Lord, your King (v. 15)
4 See, I'm doing a new thing! (v. 19)
5 I, even I, blot out your transgressions (v. 25)
6 I'll pour out my Spirit on your offspring (Isaiah 44:3)

For these notes I rely on Bible commentators for their wisdom and insights. For the six themes I looked to Barry Webb, *The Message of Isaiah* (Inter-Varsity Press, 1996). Let's enjoy God's word together!

Don't fear

'Do not fear, for I have redeemed you; I have summoned you by name; you are mine. When you pass through the waters, I will be with you; and when you pass through the rivers, they will not sweep over you.' (vv. 1–2, NIV)

Welcome to the book of Isaiah! It's been called a miniature Bible, because just as the Bible has 66 books, the message of Isaiah has 66 chapters. All the Bible's major themes appear here, including judgement and hope. We're exploring from its second part, which starts at chapter 40 and is known as the book of comfort, or the book of consolation.

Isaiah speaks these words on God's behalf to his people in exile, those in the southern kingdom of Judah. He's warning that in the future the unthinkable will happen: they will be exiled to Babylon. They will have to leave their beloved home. They will feel that there's no coming back, but Isaiah assures them otherwise. Thus, God says to them, 'Do not fear.'

Notice how God calls his people by name; he knows them and loves them, and he enjoys their intimate and loving relationship. The original Hebrew language here has a sense of, 'Mine you are!' And so even though they face hardship and pain, passing through rivers and walking in fire, they can be assured that they won't drown or be burned, because God is with them. They need not fear.

Notice too, in verse 3, how God says that he's the Lord their God. Here he reminds them of what he called himself during the exodus, when they left Egypt for the promised land. He's calling to mind how he saved them in the past, thus implying that he will save them again.

These rich words of promise applied to God's people long ago, and I believe he means them for us too. Might you personalise them today, speaking them over yourself as if God speaks them over you? I pray that you'll know his loving assurances, believing that the waters won't pass over you.

Loving God, you promise that the fires won't burn me and the rivers won't wash over me. You will be with me because you have redeemed me. Help me to know these truths not only in my head but also in my heart. Amen.

AMY BOUCHER PYE

I love you

Since you are precious and honoured in my sight, and because I love you, I will give people in exchange for you, nations in exchange for your life. Do not be afraid, for I am with you; I will bring your children from the east and gather you from the west. (vv. 4–5, NIV)

Despairing, Carolyn asked God to show her how much he loved her. As she leafed through the pages of the Bible, she stopped in Isaiah. Hardly believing her eyes, she read the words of this passage through tears: 'Since you are precious and honoured in my sight, and because I love you…' (v. 4). 'I love you,' she sensed God saying to her. 'I love you.'

When Isaiah uttered these words to God's people on God's behalf, they were recorded in Hebrew in the perfect tense – meaning that God's love for his people continues; it's ongoing. Love is the unchanging nature of God. How amazing is that? Even the grammar in the original language makes it clear that God loved his people to whom these words were spoken, and he loves Carolyn, and he loves you and me.

God then repeats what he said earlier – do not be afraid (v. 5). Although they may be exiled to Babylon, they've experienced exile in Egypt previously. God rescued them before, so can't they believe that he will come for them again?

Then God affirms again that they are his people and he is their God, they are called by his name, and they are made by him (v. 7). Because he's created them, he won't abandon them. They shouldn't fear.

When we truly know that God loves us – when that love bookends our days, when we receive this love right when we wake and before we fall asleep – we are changed. We're able to trust God in our times of challenge, when perhaps we're not living where we wish we could be (as was the experience of God's people of old). Knowing that God created us and loves us, we feel secure and safe, no matter our outward circumstances. I pray that's true for you today.

Creator God, you love me! You've made me and you're my God. Help me to embrace this truth when I waver in my belief or when all of the stuff of my life seems to point otherwise. You love me! Amen.

AMY BOUCHER PYE

My witnesses

'You are my witnesses,' declares the Lord, 'and my servant whom I have chosen, so that you may know and believe me and understand that I am he. Before me no god was formed, nor will there be one after me.' (v. 10, NIV)

With these verses, and the few before this passage, we've entered a courtroom scene. God, through Isaiah, puts himself in the dock with his people. After all, God says, which of the other gods foretold what would happen? Let those gods bring their witnesses to prove that they were right (v. 9). God observes that these gods can't prove it, but he knows that his people can – *you* are my witnesses, he says. God's people might be wracked with fear while in exile, but they have seen what God can do and how he can save. Thus, he assures them, they are his witnesses.

Continuing with the persuasive courtroom speech, God repeats in verse 11 that he's the Lord, the Saviour. This is not the role, he stresses, of some foreign god. Unlike them, God reveals and saves and proclaims, and his people are his witnesses. They may be limited, but they can attest on his behalf as to who he is.

This truth remains today. Have you, for instance, heard the saying, made popular through St Teresa of Ávila that God has no other hands but ours? I find it amazing that God would entrust his saving message to the likes of me – but then I remember that his Spirit lives in me, giving me the words to speak to others. When God lovingly prompts me, a friend or family member comes to mind, and when I contact them, I'm amazed to learn that it was just that moment when they were feeling low and needing encouragement.

How might you be God's witness today? How could you share about how he's at work in your life?

Lord God, please show me how I can bear witness to your love and leading in my life. Help me to be alert and aware of your presence within me. I know you love to love others through me. Amen.

AMY BOUCHER PYE

The Lord, the King

'For your sake I will send to Babylon and bring down as fugitives all the Babylonians, in the ships in which they took pride. I am the Lord, your Holy One, Israel's Creator, your King.' (vv. 14–15, NIV)

Trouble is looming ahead for God's people; he's cautioning them over travails to come, namely with Babylon, this foreign power. (This is the first mention specifically of Babylon by name in this second half of the book of Isaiah.) But with the warning God also reminds them of who *he* is – his power, his holiness, his character. Their enemy is not on an equal footing with him. He reveals this truth through the names he lists to remind them of his stature: your Redeemer, the Holy One of Israel, Israel's Creator, your King. God wants them to believe that he's more powerful than the powers in Babylon. Although this foreign power will affect them, they won't be lost forever.

Then in verses 16–17 he reminds his people of how they escaped the Egyptians in the Red Sea. The impossible happened – the waters parted and they crossed on dry land, even through the 'mighty waters'. Their then enemy, whom they feared, was no match for their God. And so again, God implies.

We rarely know what trouble may lie ahead for us, and sometimes we fear the future and its unknown. But then when the future becomes the present, we see that what we feared might happen didn't, but other things did. In our fear we too can land on the truths that God shared with his people through Isaiah, that he is our Redeemer, our Creator, the Holy One. He's bigger and more powerful than all the opponents we face (whether actual people or such things as discouragement, gossip, disease and so on). He won't ever leave us; we need not fear. He's the Lord.

Holy God, you are mighty and all-powerful, and yet you adore me. Thank you for your love and your promise never to leave me. Help me to receive your assurances of protection, care and companionship. Amen.

AMY BOUCHER PYE

A new thing

'Forget the former things; do not dwell on the past. See, I am doing a new thing! Now it springs up; do you not perceive it? I am making a way in the wilderness and streams in the wasteland.' (vv. 18–19, NIV)

As I mentioned in January, my family and I will be moving from north to southwest London. It feels a wrench to leave this part of our beloved city, and at times I can be tempted to lean on my memories of our years here instead of trusting God about where he is calling us. These verses from centuries ago help me to put my trust in the God of the new.

Here, God makes a promise to his people about the new thing he'll be doing in saving them from Babylon – even *before* they are exiled there. They will face difficulty and heartache, but he tells them not to focus on the past. Rather, he invites them to perceive the new thing that he will bring forth, the seemingly impossible feat of making a stream in the desert.

God's people were exiled later and then did return to Jerusalem to rebuild the temple, as we saw in January when we journeyed through the book of Haggai. They faced discouragement as they looked on the ruins of the temple, their once beloved home for God. But to hold on to hope in God, they could have hearkened back to these encouraging words of Isaiah from over 200 years before. God equipped them in advance.

This prophecy applies to the work of God through Jesus, too, and our final home in the new heaven and the new earth. God is always doing a new thing in our lives; he's the God of redemption and fresh starts. We might fear the future – such as in embracing a new church and home community – but we can keep his promises close to our hearts, knowing that he is true to his word. He is doing a new thing.

God of the new, turn my eyes to you and help me to believe your promises – not only in my head, but also with my heart. I want to believe; please strengthen my faith in you. Amen.

AMY BOUCHER PYE

Blotting out our sins

'But you have burdened me with your sins and wearied me with your offences. I, even I, am he who blots out your transgressions, for my own sake, and remembers your sins no more.' (vv. 24–25, NIV)

God is holy and therefore cannot tolerate our sins. He calls his people to account, naming how they have failed him – they've not brought him offerings or wearied themselves for him. Instead, they've worn him down with their sins and offences. Although God called them to himself, they ignored him. They got on with their own agendas and projects... Sound familiar?

We can read this passage and feel more and more burdened and guilty as we relate to God's people of old. We too have let God down – we haven't turned to him with true repentance nor offered him our finest work. However, notice the verse in the middle which brims with redemption: God, for his own sake, stamps out the record of our wrongdoing. He remembers our sins no longer; they are erased, removed (v. 25).

We see at the end of this passage how God involves his people again, inviting them to continue the courtroom scene of reviewing their past together (v. 26). If we didn't move into Isaiah 44 (as we will tomorrow), we might feel crestfallen as we consider the list of sins against God and his actions in response. God is holy and the wrongdoing against him must be paid for, but as we will see tomorrow, God will take care of that through his plan.

What wrongdoing has God blotted out for you? You might wish to spend some time with God, reviewing the past together, seeing if his Spirit gently brings to mind anything you'd like to share with him. He will free you from your sin and give you the gift of his cleansing, living water, even as he does for me. May it be so.

Forgiving God, thank you for sending your Son to take on my burdens, that I might be free of my wrongdoing. Help me to embrace this freedom as I share your love and your life with others. Amen.

AMY BOUCHER PYE

God's Spirit on us

'Do not be afraid, Jacob, my servant, Jeshurun, whom I have chosen. For I will pour water on the thirsty land, and streams on the dry ground; I will pour out my Spirit on your offspring, and my blessing on your descendants.' (vv. 2–3, NIV)

We move into the first verses of the next chapter because they tie up so well the themes we've been exploring. Here Isaiah repeats God's statements to his people, namely that he's made and formed them, that he's chosen them and that he'll help them (vv. 1–2). Sensing their anxiety, he tells them not to be afraid.

Then we reach a wonderful climax, one that would have given God's people hope when Isaiah first spoke it. This promise reverberates for us today too, that God will pour out his blessing – his Spirit – on our offspring. Not only will we receive his refreshment in our dry and thirsty times, but he also promises not to abandon our loved ones either. God's promises are not only for now, but also for our children and our children's children. What riches! What glorious promises!

We've seen deep and wonderful themes in this portion of Isaiah. Let's summarise: God assures his people that he is theirs and they are his; in fact, he's made a covenant with them. He's forgiven them, releasing them from any penalty. He continues to act in their lives. They can rely on his word.

God intends these truths not only for his people of old, but also for us. We only need to believe. If that's challenging, we can ask the Holy Spirit to help us, and he will answer. So, in closing, I pray that you can trust in God, whatever changes or things loom in your future, even as I hold on to the hope in his word. May he drench our dry ground with his living, refreshing water.

Lord Jesus, in you flow springs of living water. Dwell within me through your Holy Spirit, that I might share this life-giving source with others. Strengthen my faith in you, that I might not waver. I love you. Amen.

AMY BOUCHER PYE

What the Bible says about tears

Jenny Sanders writes...

One day, when I was about six or seven years old, the happy thought came to me: 'I don't think I've cried at all today.' Tears must have featured regularly for me to have felt the lack of them so profoundly. Maybe I was a cry-baby; as the youngest of three, I was regularly thwarted trying to keep up with my sisters, so crying was an effective way to express my frustration.

Why do we cry? What's the point of tears?

Science says we have three different types of tears: basal tears, reflex tears and emotional tears. The water/salt fluid comes from lacrimal glands above our eyes, and the oily part from the meibomian glands along our eyelash line. Blinking washes the solution across our eye, helping lubricate it, healing any damage on the surface and ensuring that light refracts correctly so we can see clearly. Tears drain away down our tear ducts. So far, so scientific; but tears do more than serve a physiological purpose.

Tears can be cathartic, signifying grief, fear, guilt, anger or shame. Tears can be an expression of joy and happiness, of attachment and overwhelm, of compassion and a broken heart, or of conviction – as the Holy Spirit speaks to us – and repentance. They can come out of deep prayer from our heart (intercession). Tears can be healing, since they contain both oxytocin and endorphins – feel-good chemicals that ease physical and emotional pain, bringing us a sense of calm. However, tears can also be self-indulgent, sentimental or manipulative; a reaction to not getting our own way. Tears can be many things, but they are God-given – an expression of the heart.

Matthew 5:4 promises that we will be comforted in mourning and grief. Ecclesiastes 3:4 tells us that there is 'a time to weep and a time to laugh, a time to mourn and a time to dance' (NIV). We can simultaneously feel strong yet opposing emotions, which is exhausting. I lost a dear friend recently, yet amid weeping I found myself laughing as I remembered some of her amusing character traits.

Why do we feel embarrassed by our tears? In the west, crying in public is frowned on, yet we live in a world where God allows us to weep. Sometimes crying is highly appropriate. Over the next fortnight, we're going to explore this topic and connect with some biblical characters who were very familiar with tears. Trust me, it won't be miserable!

God sees our tears

As she sat there, she began to sob. God heard the boy crying, and the angel of God called to Hagar from heaven and said to her, 'What is the matter, Hagar? Do not be afraid; God has heard the boy crying as he lies there.' (vv. 16–17, NIV)

Have you ever been so overwhelmed that you've literally lain down and cried? Not a few leaked tears trickling down your cheeks, but earth-shattering, body-shuddering, breath-stopping sobbing? I hope not, but you won't be alone if you have. Life can strike some bitter blows.

When things seem dark, desperate and hopeless, it's natural to feel overwhelmed. Our bodies can flood with adrenaline and the emotional part of our brain (limbic) overrides the analytical, logical, interpretive part (the frontal cortex), leaving us feeling foggy and struggling to join our thoughts up to make any sense. Tears can serve as a pressure valve in stressful moments, a way to clean up and process our experience.

For Hagar, whom Abram's wife Sarai had volunteered as a surrogate, life as she knew it had ground to a halt. Far from being the answer to the old couple's problem, once Isaac – the child of promise – was born, she and her son became inconvenient irritants to her mistress. Eventually Sarai demanded that Hagar be banished from the family. She was sent off into the desert with Ishmael and with limited supplies for their survival.

Her situation was pitiful. Hagar's tears were probably a mix of desperation and frustrated despair; a reaction to the injustice and ignominy of her drastic change of circumstances. With no solution on her limited horizon, she assumed that they would both die in the wilderness.

However, God saw her as he had once before (Genesis 16:15), heard her son crying and responded to them, supplying their needs and leading them on into his promises (16:12; 21:18). Ishmael's name means 'God hears' – a permanent reminder of God's kindness.

In the same way, God not only sees our tears but also comes to wipe them away and bring us hope.

Loving heavenly Father, thank you that you don't just observe my tears from afar; you come close and bring your kindness and consolation to me in the midst of sorrow. Help me to be aware of your closeness today. Amen.

JENNY SANDERS

Message in a bottle

You keep track of all my sorrows. You have collected all my tears in your bottle. You have recorded each one in your book. (Psalm 56:8, NLT)

I wonder what prompted King David to write Psalm 6. It's a mixture of deep sorrow and penitence. Perhaps it's an expression of heartbreak over his son Absalom's treachery and death (2 Samuel 15—18) or his own sin with Bathsheba (2 Samuel 11). Either way, his heart and mind are so burdened that he feels it even in his bones (v. 2).

In Psalm 56, David asks God for mercy, shoring up his faith by declaring that he will choose to continue to trust God in the face of fear. While he asks God to deal with his enemies, David requests that he 'list my tears on your scroll' (v. 8, NIV) or note them down in a book.

Why would God do that? Here are two possible reasons. I like the image of God collecting and keeping our tears in a bottle (NLT, above). It evokes ship-wrecked Robinson Crusoe sealing a written message in a bottle and hurling it out to sea in the desperate hope that a rescuer will find it and respond. Second, bottles are still used by cooks in the summer months to preserve fruit for use during the long, cold European winters.

God is both our rescuer and our preserver. To keep a record of our tears, or even to store racks of them on metaphorical shelves, is a powerful picture of someone who deems the contents to be special. Because we're precious to God, so are our tears. Honest outpourings of what lies in our hearts carry unquantifiable value to him. Tears carry meaning that words can't always express.

In parallel with knowing how many hairs are on my head (Matthew 10:30), keeping my tears as an act of compassionate remembrance tells me that God is the God of detail and infinite love.

Thank you for the reminder today that you care for me far more deeply than I am usually aware. Thank you for knowing every detail of my life in both sorrow and joy, and for being consistently for me. Amen.

JENNY SANDERS

Esau's tears

See that no one is sexually immoral, or is godless like Esau, who for a single meal sold his inheritance rights as the oldest son. Afterwards, as you know, when he wanted to inherit this blessing, he was rejected. Even though he sought the blessing with tears, he could not change what he had done. (Hebrews 12:16–17, NIV)

The sibling rivalry between twins Esau and Jacob began early. Genesis 25:22 says 'the babies jostled each other' inside Rebekah's womb. We probably sympathise: vastly pregnant and deeply uncomfortable, she brought her pain to God. He told her that, against cultural tradition, her older son would serve the younger. Conflict was inevitable.

The boys were of different appearances and temperaments, but Esau's tears came years later. He made a foolish blunder when he sold his precious birthright to his brother for the price of a bowl of stew. Carelessly casting it off indicated a lack of respect or understanding for his position in the family. Rather than enjoy the long-term, inherent benefits of the first-born son, Esau opted for the short-term pleasure of a quick meal.

Later still, his father Isaac wanted to bless Esau before he passed away. Sneaky Jacob, with help from his mother (who shows us the perils of favouritism), disguised himself as Esau, fooled his father and stole the blessing which was rightfully his brother's (Genesis 27:28–29). When Esau realised the trick, his frustration at this second loss brought him to furious tears (Genesis 27:34–38). Esau despised his inheritance but wanted the blessing. Do we do the same?

As children of God, our birthright includes being part of God's family. We have intrinsic significance, forgiveness, new life, the Holy Spirit inside us and access to all the resources of heaven. What a privilege! But, constantly craving warm feelings from the attention or affirmation of others, personal 'words', material possessions or self-centred priorities, can make us undervalue the lavish kindness of God in what we've already been given. Let's rejoice in his generosity and goodness today.

Lord Jesus, please forgive me for the times I've behaved like Esau. Thank you, Holy Spirit, that I can enjoy both birthright and blessing in my heavenly Father's house each day. Amen.

JENNY SANDERS

Tears of loss

'My face is red with weeping, dark shadows ring my eyes... my eyes pour out tears to God.' (vv. 16, 20, NIV)

Even in the secular world, Job is the epitome of personal devastation – the man who lost everything, including his health. Only his bitter wife remained, exacerbating his misery with her cruel words (Job 1:9–10). The phrase 'Job's comforters' describes those who fail to show compassion or empathy. Perhaps you've met them? Job's pain was emotional, physical and spiritual, yet he remained aware of God.

Crying for what we've lost is the healthy way to navigate grief. God remains in charge, still works all things together for the good of those who love him (Romans 8:28) and so on, but, inevitably, we wrestle with these truths in dark times. They serve as a crucible for growing our spiritual muscle as we choose to lean into God's promises.

Being told your loved one has gone 'somewhere better' may be theologically correct, but in a place of raw pain it can sound hollow. Acknowledging injustice, loss, the breaking up of relationships and deaths that mark the end of a life-chapter is important. The tears we shed are cathartic, an important part of the grieving process. They allow us to honour those people, recognising the impact and place they have had in our lives.

Job experienced spiritual pain too. He was baffled by God's apparent absence, confused by his suffering and questioned why disaster had come to his door. Appealing to his own integrity, he went through a crisis of faith.

No words could ease this, but the path of sorrow led to an encounter with God that changed Job's relationship with him from cognitive and distant to personal and real (Job 42:5). Despite never receiving an answer for why any of these tragedies had happened, Job realised that rather than rely on his own track record of integrity, he could have a personal relationship with God.

Father, I am grateful that because of Jesus, I can know you for myself rather than just know about you. Help me to trust you in times of trial as my faith grows and your name is glorified. Amen.

JENNY SANDERS

Tears of heartache

In her deep anguish Hannah prayed to the Lord, weeping bitterly. (v. 10, NIV)

Hannah's grief came not from something that had happened but from something which hadn't happened. The uneasy role of second wife was made more miserable as Penninah gloated over her own fruitfulness, provoking Hannah with snide remarks and jibes that caused deep hurt. We can understand Hannah's tears.

Consumed with grief over her inability to conceive, Hannah wisely took her sorrow to God in prayer during an annual visit to Shiloh. She wasn't there to make a scene but to express the anguished overflow of her bruised heart. This was an issue between her and God. The agony of it rendered her speechless. While her lips moved, it was Hannah's heart that cried out to God even as her tears fell.

Here is authentic heartache. Hannah's distress before God held nothing back and was thoroughly misinterpreted by Eli, the priest.

I believe that God is looking for authenticity in every part of our lives, whether we're celebrating, sobbing, wrestling through issues, building relationships, filled with regret or flat on our face aching for our circumstances to change. Since we can't hide from God, opening our hearts to him in transparent honesty is the best thing we can do.

What do you grieve for? A parent, a partner, your children, a career, an opportunity? Perhaps the enemy has stolen something from you which has altered your life trajectory. God may not give you the answer you want, but he promises to be with you in the struggle.

Hannah's yearning for a child was answered with baby Samuel, who became one of Israel's greatest prophetic leaders, ushering in the era of monarchy. Bitter rivalry was transformed into something beautiful. Not only that, but Hannah went on to have three more sons and two daughters (1 Samuel 2:21) bringing both comfort and consolation.

Gracious Father, you know me inside out; I can't even hide my thoughts from you. Thank you that you know and care about the things that bother me. Give me courage to always talk to you. Amen.

JENNY SANDERS

Tears of exhaustion

When David and his men reached Ziklag, they found it destroyed by fire and their wives and sons and daughters taken captive. So David and his men wept aloud until they had no strength left to weep. (vv. 3–4, NIV)

There's a backstory here. David and his 600 men had sheltered with Achish, the King of Gath, in Philistine territory for 16 months – respite from being pursued by King Saul. Achish provided the town of Ziklag so they could settle. It was all going smoothly until the Philistines joined together for a military excursion. They objected to David's entourage, fearing a double-cross was afoot and they'd be betrayed in the midst of battle.

Thoroughly fed up, David was ordered to take his men and leave – a humiliating exit. A three-day journey took them home, only to find that the Amalekites had burned Ziklag to the ground and captured all the people: their wives, sons and daughters. A brutal body-blow, so soon after the first disappointment and on top of physical exhaustion, fed into unbridled rage, despair and an outpouring of tears.

David's men were so angry they threatened to stone him. What could he do? Verse 6 says: 'David found strength in the Lord his God.' I once heard this explained as: 'David introduced himself to himself.' Despite feeling completely wrung out, David chose to reconnect, or plug back into, God – his source of strength and hope. He reminded himself of the faithfulness and promises of God and his own calling. While he had no physical or emotional strength left, he spoke truth to his soul.

Consequently, under the guidance of another godly man, David became convinced that God had further plans which didn't end in the ashes of Ziklag. Regrouping his men, they pursued the Amalekites and subsequently rescued every person who had been taken.

Are you overwhelmed by disappointment today? Perhaps you have cried yourself to a place of exhaustion and can see no hope for the future. Like David, take your hurt to God in prayer.

Remind yourself today of the truths God has highlighted. Reflect on his promises again and allow the Holy Spirit to give you strength for the next step. Trust him for the journey, from weeping in the ashes to unshakeable joy.

JENNY SANDERS

The language of lament

My eyes fail from weeping, I am in torment within; my heart is poured out on the ground because my people are destroyed, because children and infants faint in the streets of the city. (Lamentations 2:11, NIV)

Lament features heavily in the Bible. An entire book is given over to this form of sorrow-filled prayer, compiled by Jeremiah ('the weeping prophet') to chronicle the pain and heartbreak of Israel after the Babylonian destruction of Jerusalem in 586BC. Despite prophetic warnings, God's people had consistently refused to listen to his correction and sought their pleasures elsewhere, including in indulging in idol worship. Jeremiah was tasked with the fruitless job of calling them back to God.

Some psalms were written as laments too: personal (e.g. 77, 142) and corporate (e.g. 44, 74, 80); all of them call on God to act. The writers express their heartache for immediate circumstances which are far from those which would please God. There's a sense of mourning and regret; a yearning to return to life lived under God's blessing and protection, whether for an individual or a nation. Reading them, we feel a spiritual heaviness; dismay that things are seriously out of joint with how they were designed to be.

Lament is as relevant as ever. We can usefully incorporate it into our walk with God. Who doesn't feel sorrow when we see the fractured world around us? Our hearts break when we witness the deliberate abandonment of God's ways among people we love and the consequent pain that brings to themselves, as well as to us. There's not a person alive who doesn't want to know real love, joy, peace and affirmation. It grieves us when we see people turn to anything except towards God to find it and then watch their hope shatter in long-term disappointment.

Lament can help us to unburden ourselves; to pray intentionally; to intercede for our world, nation, town and family; and to see circumstances from God's perspective and cry out for his mercy and love.

Hope is the antidote to despair: 'May the God of hope fill you with all joy and peace as you trust in him, so that you may overflow with hope by the power of the Holy Spirit' (Romans 15:13).

JENNY SANDERS

Night-time tears

For his anger lasts only a moment, but his favour lasts a lifetime; weeping may stay for the night, but rejoicing comes in the morning. (v. 5, NIV)

It's never a good idea to make decisions after midnight. If, like me, you've been awake at 3.00 am contemplating a situation for which you can see no solution, you'll know that sense of utter hopelessness which can trigger tears. Everything is bleak at that time; our brains are foggy, our frontal cortex (logic) is not fully operational, but our imaginations seem on hyper-alert, endlessly considering the 'What if…' scenarios and finding only gloom-laden answers.

Research suggests that most hospital deaths occur between 3.00 am and 4.00 am, when hope is at a low ebb. It's the time when we are most vulnerable; our bodies are short of adrenaline and our brains are trying to file yesterday's problems in readiness for the challenges of a new day.

But morning is coming! Everything looks better by daylight. We think more rationally, can confer with others, banish those night-time bogeymen and embrace the realities of the day with confidence and competence.

That doesn't mean that our worries disappear like morning mist, but we're more likely to remember that God knows and has both seen and heard us. I love the reassurance of Psalm 34:18: 'The Lord is close to the broken-hearted and saves those who are crushed in spirit.' For those of us familiar with night-time tears, we have the promise that God himself is near to us.

Tears are for a season, not forever. They can take us on a cathartic journey towards comfort, restoration, encouragement, fresh strength and replenishment. Crying can be restorative; it's part of the way we are designed by God. Tears have a purpose.

Psalm 126:5 says: 'Those who sow with tears will reap with songs of joy.' Perhaps our night-time tears are an investment, when we include God in our thinking, which can bring 'returns' of comfort and delight.

Thank you, heavenly Father, that you are with me through the night as well as the day. Help me to listen for your voice when my thoughts feel scrambled. Help me to know your peace when night-time tears flow. Amen.

JENNY SANDERS

Perfumed tears

A woman in that town who lived a sinful life… as she stood behind [Jesus] at his feet weeping, she began to wet his feet with her tears. Then she wiped them with her hair, kissed them and poured perfume on them. (vv. 37–38, NIV)

We don't know much about this woman. Luke records the fact that she had 'lived a sinful life,' which was usually a reference to immorality. There is no explanation as to how she knew that Jesus was having supper with this particular Pharisee nor what boldness drew her there.

Presumably, she had either heard about Jesus or was among a crowd who listened to him preach somewhere. Perhaps she'd witnessed him healing someone or maybe she'd seen the change in another woman with a reputation: Mary Magdalene. Whatever the background story, the fact that despite her notoriety she entered the house of one of the religious elite tells us that she was desperate. Had she been discovered earlier, she would have been unceremoniously thrown out.

2 Corinthians 7:10 tells us that 'godly sorrow brings repentance'. More than regret, this type of sorrow inspires change and contains hope – not in our ability to turn over a new leaf, but in the power of Jesus' death and resurrection to heal the rift between us and God. The Greek word is *penthos*: a passage through grief over wrongdoing which leads us to the releasing joy of forgiveness and reconciliation with God – an idea central to Eastern Orthodox faith and embodied by this woman with her special perfume.

Tears can be a natural reaction in the presence of holiness, as we become aware of our own heart state and flawed humanity, the outward manifestation of what's happening inside us.

Through her fragrant tears, this woman heard that she was forgiven, saved and could 'go in peace' (v. 50). Jesus restored her dignity, her hope and ensured she was properly seen in a room full of men where culture insisted they ignore her. Surely her tears turned to joy. So can ours.

Loving Saviour, thank you for the wonder of forgiveness. Lord Jesus, I am so grateful that while I cannot change myself, you are more than able to. Thank you, Holy Spirit, for your power that is making me more like Jesus. Amen.

JENNY SANDERS

Crocodile tears

All the people were wailing and mourning for her. (v. 52, NIV)

I have four grown-and-flown children, and I cannot imagine the devastation of losing any of them. Jairus' daughter was on the verge of adolescence; her hopes and dreams evaporating as sickness stole her life away.

By the time he brought Jesus home, professional mourners had been hired, ensuring that the whole neighbourhood was alerted without the family having to go through the exhausting necessity of repeatedly verbalising their loss.

However, these tears were just that: a job. Mourners went through the motions of weeping and wailing – 'crocodile tears' – not the authentic personal reaction to the loss of a much-loved daughter, which doubtless had been going on behind closed doors for Jairus' wife. See how quickly their cries and clamour turned to laughter when Jesus arrived. 'Stop wailing,' he commanded. 'She is not dead but asleep' (v. 52).

I'm so glad that Jesus responded to Jairus, not to the crowd with their insincere tears. He saw how Jairus, a respected synagogue leader, had humbled himself to come and seek help from the itinerant preacher; how he'd been forced to wait while another woman of faith, who the law said shouldn't even be out in public, was graciously healed. Jairus kept his eyes on Jesus. He may have wobbled when the news came that his daughter had died but, with Jesus' encouragement, he didn't crumble.

With just five other people in the room, Jesus spoke authoritative resurrection life. He didn't need the razzmatazz of a big audience before intervening. No wonder Jairus and his wife were 'astonished' (v. 56) to receive their daughter back from the dead. Now I'm certain they cried: tears of relief and gratitude.

Tears don't always tell us what's happening inside someone, but God sees the truth; he knows our hearts.

Have there been times when you used tears to give an impression of something that wasn't truly so? Ask God for forgiveness and pray for discernment so that you can react appropriately to the tears of others.

JENNY SANDERS

Jesus wept too

During the days of Jesus' life on earth, he offered up prayers and petitions with fervent cries and tears to the one who could save him from death, and he was heard because of his reverent submission. (Hebrews 5:7, NIV)

I find it comforting to know that Jesus cried real tears, just like me. It reminds me that while fully God, he was also fully human. His tears reveal compassion, grief, pain and distress. They're revealed when Jesus cried over Jerusalem as he lamented the people's stubborn refusal to recognise God's plan and foresaw its coming destruction in AD70 (Luke 19:41), and again during his sweat-inducing intercession in Gethsemane before his crucifixion (Matthew 26:38; Mark 14:33).

Our passage today tells how Jesus stood outside his friend Lazarus's tomb and wept, even though he was about to raise him from the dead. Does it strike you as strange?

Jesus had delayed his visit to Bethany even though a message informed him of his friend's illness. Clearly, it's not that Jesus didn't care; he could see a bigger picture of God's hand and the glory that would come to his Father through this situation (v. 5).

However, witnessing the palpable grief of both Martha and Mary and empathising with their raw and conflicting emotions, Jesus felt the weight of the impact death has on us all. The finality of a life cut off is a shattering jolt; we are seldom ready to accept it. Jesus also knew that death was not part of God's original design but a consequence of Adam and Eve's disobedience (Genesis 3). Cut to the heart by what sin has done to us all, it's less surprising that he wept.

Loss takes us to the end of ourselves. Words fail to comfort us, which is why Paul's advice was to: 'Rejoice with those who rejoice; mourn with those who mourn' (Romans 12:15). When we're bereft and out of words, tears are our friends. Jesus knows and understands this.

Lord Jesus, I thank you that you are the resurrection and the life. Please comfort those who are grieving over the loss of loved ones today. Thank you that in you we have eternal hope. Amen.

JENNY SANDERS

Tears of regret

Then Peter remembered the word Jesus had spoken: 'Before the cock crows, you will disown me three times.' And he went outside and wept bitterly. (v. 75, NIV)

Peter, the brashest, boldest and most impetuous of Jesus' followers, had a night he would remember forever. After boasting that he was better than all the rest who might well fall away, he declared he would never let Jesus down. He even bravely waved a sword around in the garden of Gethsemane and nearly took someone's head off (fishermen weren't used to handling weapons!). Yet, just a few hours later, he's reduced to a stammering, lying wreck by a servant girl around a fire.

Luke records poignantly how when the cock crowed, 'The Lord turned and looked straight at Peter' (Luke 22:61). What did that look convey? Rebuke? Possibly. I think it was more likely to have been a combination of sorrow and deep, undying love. Every time Peter heard a cockerel for the rest of his life, this moment must have replayed in his memory.

Not only had he, like the rest, run away when soldiers arrested Jesus in the garden, but he also subsequently pretended he didn't even know him; not once but three times. He made a deliberate choice to deny his Lord. The bitter tears of regret must have come with a sobering re-estimation of who Peter really was deep inside, and it broke him. Overwhelmed with guilt and shame, he sought solace far from the fire in the dark of a lonely night.

Been there? Most of us have, if we're honest. The question is, did we stay there? Jesus brought his friend back to the fire in a resurrection breakfast on the shores of Galilee, including an intimate chat about the substance and reality of Peter's love (John 21).

What grace! What forgiveness! What restoration! Peter didn't stay wallowing in self-pity and self-recrimination. Somewhere, regret became remorse, then repentance and, finally, restoration.

Has regret, bitterness or self-loathing robbed you of God's good plans? Take some time now to unload any such burdens and enjoy his transforming grace again today. He is eager to meet you with forgiveness, comfort and love.

JENNY SANDERS

Tears of joy

He asked her, 'Woman, why are you crying?' (v. 15, NIV)

Resurrection morning hadn't fully dawned when Mary Magdalene went to the garden grave. Having taken baffling news of the empty tomb to the disciples, her aimless feet took her back there.

Bewildered, confused, heartbroken and bereft, she wept for the one who had irrevocably changed her life, delivered her from torment and healed her pain. They were tears of unspeakable loss. Emboldened by John and Peter's action, Mary ducked her head through the doorway to check for herself that Jesus' body really was gone. John states matter-of-factly that two white-clothed angels sat serenely inside (v. 12).

How would you have reacted? In her emotional turmoil, Mary didn't seem to find it strange and simply answered their question about why she was crying, then turned to leave. Her vision blurred by tears, she almost bumped into someone she assumed must be the gardener. He asked the same question. Desperate for some solidity in the shifting sand of her emotions, Mary grabbed the possibility that he might know where Jesus' body might be. She just wanted to be near him again.

Then, in one of the most magnificent moments of not just the New Testament, but all of history, Jesus spoke her name: 'Mary.' Just one word and, immediately, she knew he was alive; her spirit leapt with inexpressible joy.

I suspect Mary cried all over again, a mixture of relief, delight and incredulity that overflowed from an overstretched heart, unable to find words to express herself.

Later, two disciples travelling to Emmaus engaged in a detailed Old Testament Bible study with the risen Jesus. Mary understood and believed when Jesus simply spoke her name. Her intimate relationship with Jesus wasn't cognitive but a living, joyous delight.

Jesus knows our name too and longs to meet with us in that vibrant life-giving reality.

Father God, forgive me for the times my relationship with you has become dry and distant. Holy Spirit, I ask that you reveal the risen Jesus to me again today and fill me with Mary's joy. Amen.

JENNY SANDERS

No more weeping

'He will wipe every tear from their eyes.' (v. 4, NIV)

This celebratory passage fizzes with joy.

Over the years, writers, theologians and philosophers have pondered what heaven might be like. I doubt even one has come close to what God has prepared for those who love him (John 14:3).

How wonderful that one day everything will be made new (v. 5). Broken bodies, minds and hearts will be restored as shadows and pain are banished forever.

The prospect of a totally different paradigm where death, mourning and crying are permanently excluded stirs a deep yearning within me. Although our world is fractured and stained by sin now, it will not always be that way. A new heaven and a new earth are in the heart of God, awaiting the day when all of history is wound up and we spend eternity with him. What a wonderful prospect!

Heaven is not about playing harps on fluffy clouds or interminable worship services we can't escape; it's about living in uninterrupted intimacy with our Saviour, Creator and King. We may not know all the details of what it will be like, but we can be sure that it will be perfect. Not only will we never cry again, but also there will be nothing to cry about!

This glimpse of what God has in store for us beyond our current life gives us hope. Biblical hope is solid and certain; it is 'divinely guaranteed' (Hebrews 11:1, AMP), and there can be no stronger assurance than that. In John's vision, he heard the extraordinary news that God himself will wipe the tears from our eyes. Just imagine!

We can trust God's promise and lift our heads knowing that darkness cannot last forever and that one day his kingdom will conquer all others as sadness and grief are swallowed up in eternal joy.

Read the Bible passage again. Now let the Holy Spirit stir you in worshipping Jesus in whichever way expresses your heart-response to his immeasurable love, boundless grace and the exciting prospect of seeing him face to face.

JENNY SANDERS

Recognising idols in our lives

Hannah Fytche writes...

Idols and idolatry are recurrent biblical themes. Scripture warns against idols – against trusting in false gods or placing hope in that which is not God. In the Old Testament, the language of 'idols' often refers to images or statues of foreign gods – the gods not of the Israelites, God's people, but other nations' gods. Such idols were believed to make those gods present in the world. Old Testament writers warn against trusting them: they are not God; they are not good, trustworthy and alive like the Israelites' God. They don't make God present in the world.

As early as the New Testament, the language of 'idolatry' expands to refer to a whole host of other things. It became language used to warn God's people against behaviours which don't align with God's love (see Colossians 3:5 or Ephesians 5:5). To choose such behaviours is to trust that which is not God. Such action doesn't make God present in the world.

As we consider the foreign gods warned against by Old Testament writers and the behaviours counselled against by New Testament writers, we'll explore what we might take as images of God. What might we be trusting as images of what's good, right and trustworthy which actually might not make God present but instead lead us astray?

We'll discover that warnings against idolatry encourage us to find life in God by seeking that which makes God present – and rejecting that which *seems* to make God present but actually doesn't. The work of recognising idols in our lives is the work of seeking the true and living God over, above and through all else. This work happens in the context of the journey from creation to new creation to which the Bible witnesses and which God's love enlivens. To remind us of this context, our reflections are bookended with texts from Genesis and Revelation. We come from and are returning to God. Along the way we're called to seek out – and even *be* – God's real and true image in the world, rejecting the falsity of idols which promise God but don't deliver. Let's begin with a prayer:

God, you are our beginning and our end. Our hearts are restless as they seek you. May your Holy Spirit's light show us where we're trusting in that which is not you, and may we be drawn to what really makes you present. Amen.

In the image of God

Then God said, 'Let us make mankind in our image, in our likeness, so that they may rule over the fish in the sea and the birds in the sky, over the livestock and all the wild animals, and over all the creatures that move along the ground.' (v. 26, NIV)

In the beginning the Holy Spirit hovered over deep waters and then God spoke. All came to be. God raised up people from dust and mud and called us God's images. We are made in the image of God: we image God, making God present to the world around us by being who we are created to be.

Making God present in the world looks like participating in God's work of bringing all things to life and bringing life to all things. Genesis 1:26–31 includes words in God's voice which illustrate this: people are made in God's image so that we may rule over the earth and its creatures. 'Rule over' means to care for and curate. We are made in God's image so that we may care, joining with God's work of bringing life.

Bringing life looks like so many things. For me, writing is part of how I participate in making God present. For someone else it may look like building gorgeous furniture that turns houses into homes – places where people are able to rest and be themselves with everything they need. For another person it may look like something completely different. In and through all contexts we can choose to live into the image in which we're made.

This pattern of living is good: 'God saw all that he had made, and it was very good' (v. 31). Making God present in the world is good. Yet the next part of the Genesis story (chapter 3) shows how this pattern is disrupted as people, Adam and Eve, choose to trust that which is not God. The image of God is distorted. So enters idolatry, the turn towards trusting that which appears to bring life, like Eden's forbidden fruit, but which ultimately leads to disruption, distortion and death.

God, I am made in your image, created to participate in making your life and love present. Yet in thought, word and deed, I disrupt the image in which I am made. May you continually recover your image in me. Amen.

HANNAH FYTCHE

Signposts towards the true and living God

'You shall not make for yourself an image in the form of anything in heaven above or on the earth beneath or in the waters below. You shall not bow down to them or worship them.' (vv. 4–5, NIV)

In the book of Exodus, we find God giving instructions to God's people. These instructions are like signposts which signal the way to live in order to embrace our identity as those made in God's image. Following God's signposts enables us to turn from trusting that which is not God towards the life that God delivers.

Our text offers some of those signposts, given to God's people through Moses on Mount Sinai (you can read more of his story in Exodus). They are part of the ten commandments, the first two of which speak to the work of recognising and rejecting idols and false images in our lives. While images of 'anything in heaven above or on the earth beneath or in the waters below' may have been celebrated and worshipped by people in Moses' time, God signals that though such images may appear to promise life they actually don't. Only the true and living God delivers lasting life.

What images of things in heaven, on earth and in the waters do we trust to bring us life? I sometimes have to work hard to remember that my worth and life are not grounded in how much work I complete or how successful I become through that work. Especially in busy and pressured seasons, I must remember not to make a god of productivity.

These signposts remind me instead that my worth and life are grounded in God. The real image of God in the world is in me, you and all those around us. Turning from the idol of productivity and its attendant image of success as that which brings life enables me to live into the truth that I am loved and created in God's image.

God, may I leave behind anything in which I hoped would promise life but which hasn't delivered. I fix my heart on you: with all that I am I turn my face towards yours, which is always turned to me. Amen.

HANNAH FYTCHE

Other peoples' idols

But their idols are silver and gold, made by human hands. They have mouths, but cannot speak, eyes, but cannot see. They have ears, but cannot hear, noses, but cannot smell. They have hands, but cannot feel, feet, but cannot walk, nor can they utter a sound with their throats. (vv. 4–7, NIV)

Throughout the Old Testament, there are scattered texts which contrast the Israelites' living God with the false gods or idols of other peoples. These clever pieces of rhetoric portray other people's gods as empty of power. Psalm 115 describes these idols as unable to speak, see, hear, smell, feel or walk – implying that the living God does all these. These are helpful illustrations, prompting us to recognise those things that we hope will bring us life but which are incapable of doing so. In recognising their emptiness and ineffectiveness, we find ourselves turning to the true and living God.

However, such rhetoric can be misused to 'other' other people and cultures. In contrasting the Israelites' God with other peoples' gods, Psalm 115 and similar texts established a boundary around God's people by denigrating other people's way of life. While one purpose of such texts is to turn people towards God, another outcome is to turn people away from those who are different than them. Some Bible scholars identify a strand of xenophobia in such texts.

In our present context, similar dynamics play out in situations where people are 'othered' on the basis of differences of body, politics, culture or faith. We elevate our own perspectives and denigrate others', inadvertently idolising our own convictions by calling others' convictions false or untrue.

Recognising idols, however, is not about upholding particular cultures or convictions, nor about rejecting difference. Rather, it involves reaching across boundaries and seeking what makes God present. We may find God in unexpected places: in the eyes of someone who holds a different theological stance; in the words of an agnostic poet; in the hands of someone who lives halfway around the world in a culture wholly different to ours.

God, teach me to recognise idols in my life and the world not on the basis of 'othering', but by discerning what makes you present and what doesn't. In all contexts and conversations, may you show me how to seek you. Amen.

HANNAH FYTCHE

Keep yourselves from idols

We know also that the Son of God has come and has given us understanding, so that we may know him who is true. And we are in him who is true by being in his Son Jesus Christ. He is the true God and eternal life. Dear children, keep yourselves from idols. (vv. 20–21, NIV)

John's first letter is written to some of the earliest Christ-followers, people working out what it meant to follow God in the context of the recent events of Jesus' life, death and resurrection. The conclusion to the letter is something that puzzles interpreters: instead of ending with personal greetings to the letter's recipients (as we often see with other New Testament letters), John finishes with affirmations of the purpose of the letter, instructions about sin and prayer, and a final entreaty: 'Dear children, keep yourselves from idols.'

It's an abrupt introduction, right in the final words of the letter, to the seemingly new topic of 'idols'. Some scholars interpret this as evidence that later edits were made to John's original letter. Others read it as a part of the whole letter, seeing throughout 1 John a contrast between true and false practices of following Christ, with affirmation of true practice intended as reassurance and exposure of the false as warning. To end on this warning against idols ties together themes from the whole letter.

Aside from providing a puzzling ending to this ancient New Testament letter, the mention of idols shows the concern among the earliest Christ-followers to seek out what is true and turn away from what is not. At the heart of that concern is Christ: a desire to follow Christ with the trust that Jesus Christ reveals God and makes God truly present to us.

Here we see, then, the language of 'idols' and 'idolatry' being understood anew in the context of Christ. Old Testament texts contrasted idols with God, but the New Testament witnesses to the revelation of God in Jesus Christ, so idols become that which deter people from following Christ and being in Christ – as we'll continue to see through the rest of this week.

God, give me love and wisdom when parts of scripture perplex me. May I find myself drawn to Christ in and through all things – that I may keep myself from that which I idolise and lean entirely on you, the true God. Amen.

HANNAH FYTCHE

Love God and love your neighbour

Jesus replied: '"Love the Lord your God with all your heart and with all your soul and with all your mind." This is the first and greatest commandment. And the second is like it: "Love your neighbour as yourself." All the Law and the Prophets hang on these two commandments.' (vv. 37–40, NIV)

An expert in the law asks Jesus what the greatest commandment is. Jesus' answer establishes that the greatest commandment and clearest signpost is love. Love of God and of neighbour signals the way to seek and find images of the true and living God, letting false idolatry fall away.

One way that we could read this interaction between Jesus and the expert is to see in it a contrast between the spirit and the letter of the law. While the expert sought to trip Jesus up on details (verse 35 describes the expert's motivation as 'testing' Jesus), Jesus responds by establishing love as the spirit of the law. Love guides how we interpret scripture.

I grew up in a church tradition which taught that I should prioritise a daily 'quiet time' with God involving an in-depth Bible study. This was often talked about in a way that communicated that if I didn't daily read the Bible in this way I wasn't 'Christian enough', I wouldn't know God well enough, and I'd be cut off from that which brings me life.

Hearing Jesus declare love as the greatest commandment is transformative. What if love rather than expectation guided how and when we read the Bible? What if reading scripture were not something we idolised, trusting that time spent with the Bible is what brings us life, but instead something through which we seek and find God's image? Such questions are freeing: I can read the Bible with love rather than pressure. Sometimes that looks like an in-depth Bible study; sometimes like reading devotional notes; sometimes like holding in my heart a single metaphor from scripture. Through it all there is love. The idol of 'quiet time' falls by the wayside.

Christ, show me how to love: may I live in ways that make you present. May your love also guide how I read the Bible. May I read scripture not because I must but because it's where I find you. Amen.

HANNAH FYTCHE

Whatever you do

Set your hearts on things above, where Christ is… And whatever you do, whether in word or deed, do it all in the name of the Lord Jesus, giving thanks to God the Father through him. (vv. 1, 17, NIV)

We're discovering that recognising and rejecting idols is about seeking God's image in and through our whole lives, so that we may trust the true and living God rather than that which promises life yet doesn't deliver. Today's text again comes from a letter sent to one of the earliest communities of Christ-followers, a group of people working out what it meant to follow God in the context of Christ's death and resurrection. What we learn in this text is that to follow Christ is to set our hearts on him, trusting him as the one who truly reveals God to us – letting all other behaviours therefore fall away. (See Colossians 1:15–20 for a gorgeous reflection on Christ as the image of God.)

Having called out behaviours which don't demonstrate trust in God but rather distort the image of God in people (vv. 5–11), the writer of this letter paints a picture of what life looks like when we reflect God's image and Christ in us (vv. 12–17). This second part concludes by saying: 'Whatever you do… do it all in the name of the Lord Jesus.'

I love this concluding statement – it's so freeing. It means that it's okay to love, enjoy and prioritise your job, relationships, rest or whatever else ('whatever you do') and to seek to live in Jesus' name through them. Loving and enjoying the gifts in our lives are not acts of idolatry. We can love our work *and* love God; idolising our work is when we trust our work rather than God to bring us life. Following Jesus does not erase all our affections; rather, Jesus shows us the way to live in all contexts, through whatever we do, in his freedom and love.

My heart is restless: I come from and I'm returning to you. Along the way and in all contexts, help me to set my heart on you, Christ, forsaking all that seems to promise life but doesn't deliver. Amen.

HANNAH FYTCHE

All that's gathered in love will remain

He who was seated on the throne said, 'I am making everything new!' Then he said, 'Write this down, for these words are trustworthy and true.' (v. 5, NIV)

We began our week's reflections in Genesis, the story that grounds us in the creative love of God, who has made us in God's image. We've since reflected on images and idols, discovering what it means to discern what truly makes God present in and through all contexts – so that we may let all else, anything which we falsely idolise, fall away.

We've asked for love to guide us. In this final reflection we turn to the end of the story: when John envisions in Revelation the moment when Christ returns and gathers all things to himself. This vision is like a promise which can fix that guiding love in us: we can see where we're going – and, just like where we've come from, the place we're going is good. God's dwelling place will be with us. Tears and death will be wiped away. All will be made new by Christ and the image of God in us will be restored to that good and right pattern established in the beginning. Disruption, distortion and death of that image will be buried in the past and new life will spring up. Isn't that astonishing? All will be made new.

On days when I find it hard to seek, find and trust real and true images of the living God in myself, those around me and the world, this promise gives me hope. It gives me perspective and courage for this bit in the middle, my journey of life through which I'm called to seek God. When I feel uncertain about how to live into the image of God in which I am made, I can return to this signpost pointing out the way ahead.

God, as I travel through this life seeking and discerning what truly makes you present, fix in me the promise of new life in which all that's gathered in your love will remain. May this embolden and encourage me. Amen.

HANNAH FYTCHE

Jesus: gentle and lowly

Tanya Marlow writes…

Russia's leader, Vladimir Putin, started a propaganda campaign to boost his popularity. He posted photos of himself shirtless and muscular, riding a horse or holding a rifle for hunting. Similarly, Donald Trump campaigned for office bragging of his physical strength and high testosterone levels and promising voters, 'I am your warrior… I am your retribution' (Conservative Political Action Conference, 4 March 2023).

Both men equated a stereotype of masculinity with success. It worked. In the world in which we live, the majority seem to crave leaders who are strong and boastful men, capable of violence and ready to wage war. Even in pockets of the church, this kind of toxic masculinity has crept in. American pastor Mark Driscoll notoriously has said: 'In Revelation, Jesus is a pride fighter with a tattoo down his leg, a sword in his hand and the commitment to make someone bleed. That is a guy I can worship… I cannot worship a guy I can beat up' ('7 Big Questions', *Relevant Magazine*, 28 August 2007).

Generally, the people who value powerful and arrogant men also wish women to be quiet, subservient and, above all, grateful. Perhaps this is why my first reaction to the series' title, 'Gentle and lowly', was to squirm a little, because often words like this have been weaponised against women and used to keep us in an inferior place in society. Even today, little girls are more likely to be praised for being gentle-spirited and modest, whereas little boys tend to be praised for boldness and self-confidence.

This is why Jesus is such an extraordinary and wonderful leader. If we consider all the attributes that first-century Jews, Romans and Greeks valued in a male leader, who would have ever picked 'gentle and lowly'? The Greeks prized intelligence, the Romans, military might, and there was a strong movement among the Jews that wanted violent revenge against their oppressors.

Jesus, the self-titled gentle and lowly king, is good news for both women and men. Jesus shows us a vision of humanity beyond gendered stereotypes and, above all, shows us the image of the loving, tender God who created us. This also makes it good news for those of us who feel weary and downtrodden in this life, needing comfort not chastisement. In the next two weeks, as we explore examples of Jesus' gentleness and humility, I pray it will nourish us and sooth our souls.

The power of gentleness

This took place to fulfil what was spoken through the prophet: 'Say to Daughter Zion, "See, your king comes to you, gentle and riding on a donkey, and on a colt, the foal of a donkey."' (vv. 4–5, NIV)

Was Jesus' entry into Jerusalem on a donkey a display of humility or a claim to power? It was certainly in part a declaration to be God's chosen messianic king. Jesus organised his entry into Jerusalem as a conscious fulfilment of Old Testament prophecy, particularly the prophet Zechariah: 'See, your king comes to you, gentle and riding on a donkey' (v. 5, quoting Zechariah 9:9, 'lowly and riding on a donkey'). The people duly responded by throwing down their coats as you might do to greet a king and by giving him a kingly title, 'Son of David' (vv. 8–9).

But what kind of king was this? The very next verse in Zechariah explains that the donkey contrasts with 'war-horses' and 'chariots', which will be taken away because God's chosen king 'will proclaim peace to the nations' (Zechariah 9:10). Jesus is not a war-waging despot but one who will bring peace and rule the nations with gentleness. While the crowd in Jerusalem ultimately turned against Jesus precisely because he hadn't come to fight, serving a gentle king is good news for those of us who long for peace in this violent world. Jesus' gentle peace is stronger than humanity's violence.

At a church in Liverpool, I once witnessed two huge, tough men yelling at each other as their argument threatened to turn violent. Then a church volunteer stepped in. He was small, thin and softly spoken, but he soothed them in an instant with his calm presence. He stopped the fight.

Today I am struck by the power of the world's peacemakers; paradoxically lowly and gentle while challenging the powerful and changing the world. Let's be unashamed followers of the leader on the donkey, not the war-horse.

Gentleness is powerful. To what extent do you believe this and live this out? Whenever you see rulers and celebrities arrive in limousines, reflect on Jesus' lowly transport.

TANYA MARLOW

Nothing too low for Jesus

After that, he poured water into a basin and began to wash his disciples' feet, drying them with the towel that was wrapped round him. (v. 5, NIV)

When I was a university student, I stayed over at my friend's family home for a week. At least, that was the intention. Unfortunately, I got ill with a horrible virus, had a raging temperature, and couldn't go home. No longer able to triumph in my capable status as a newly minted adult, I was entirely dependent on my friend's mother, who nursed me kindly. The lowest point came when she offered to wash my clothes for me, and after some hesitation, I handed over my sour, sweaty bundle, including my underwear. Because she was so kind, though, it turned from a moment of humiliation to a story I remember for her love.

I imagine the disciples felt something similar when they had their feet washed by Jesus. Although Jesus uses the foot-washing as a metaphor for the cleansing of our sins on the cross ('Later you will understand', v. 7), I want to focus on the lowly serving element of Jesus' actions. John reminds us of Jesus' divine, exalted status and authority ('The Father had put all things under his power', v. 3), and then contrasts that with Jesus washing the sweat, dirt and stink from the disciples' feet. No wonder Peter squirms and protests: 'No… you shall never wash my feet' (v. 8).

Through this, Jesus shows us that there is no issue too lowly, too shameful or too gross that God is not interested in helping us with. I wonder how often you unconsciously censor your prayers, thinking either that it's not important enough for God's attention or that it involves too much shame so you want to hide away. Jesus is not shocked by our dirt and sweat and wants to gently help us. He loves us to the end (v. 1).

Consider what you take to God in prayer and what you hold back. What elements of your life feel too shameful, too mundane, too unimportant or too repetitive to entrust to Jesus? Tenderly entrust them to him today.

TANYA MARLOW

Comfort for overwhelmed souls

He took Peter, James and John along with him, and he began to be deeply distressed and troubled. 'My soul is overwhelmed with sorrow to the point of death', he said to them. 'Stay here and keep watch.' (vv. 33–34, NIV)

Most days, because of my chronic illness, I am confined to my bed. This means I have to ask friends to visit me rather than go to their house. They need to test beforehand for Covid, and when they arrive, they have to make the tea rather than me making it for them. Whenever I am tempted to tell myself, 'I am too needy' or 'My situation is too much for others' and start to blame myself, I think of Jesus at Gethsemane.

Anticipating his death, Jesus was vulnerable and emotionally needy, and 'he began to be deeply distressed and troubled' (v. 33). At times of distress, it is normal and natural to need others to comfort, console or protect us. Jesus – God incarnate – pleaded to his closest friends, 'My soul is overwhelmed with sorrow to the point of death… Stay here and keep watch' (v. 34). Tragically, they let him down, repeatedly falling asleep instead of keeping a lookout for enemies (vv. 37, 40, 41).

Jesus was simultaneously God's celebrated king and a vulnerable human. At Gethsemane, Jesus shows us that no one is so exalted in this world that they don't need emotional support from others, and no one is so low in this world's hierarchy that they don't deserve comfort in hard times.

If Jesus needed friends to be with him in a stressful situation, we certainly do, too. If you are feeling unworthy of love and support, take courage from Jesus' vulnerability, loneliness and boldness in asking for help. Likewise, if you have been let down by friends when you needed them most, draw comfort in Jesus' understanding of that great pain. Finally, may we all aspire to be friends who 'watch and pray' (v. 38).

Lord Jesus, when I am at my lowest, please give me friends who will watch and pray. Give me the boldness to ask, and give them the grace to accept. In my distress, Lord, comfort my soul. Amen.

TANYA MARLOW

When darkness reigns

When Jesus' followers saw what was going to happen, they said, 'Lord, should we strike with our swords?' And one of them struck the servant of the high priest, cutting off his right ear. But Jesus answered, 'No more of this!' And he touched the man's ear and healed him. (vv. 49–51, NIV)

If the gospels were a blockbuster action movie, this would be the moment for the triumphant battle – a rag-tag bunch of good-hearted, untrained nobodies who unite as a team, fighting against the whole of Judas' armed mob. Boom! Some well-aimed punches, plus kung-fu moves from Peter, and Jesus hurries on victorious.

The reality, though, is rather more pathetic. Jesus' followers don't have a clue what to do: 'Lord, should we strike with our swords?' (v. 49). In the uncertainty, 'one of them' (identified as Peter in John's gospel), makes a defiant strike to fight back – but all he achieves is cutting off the ear of the high priest's servant (v. 50), which is not a move that will win a battle.

Luke's gospel is the only account that tells of Jesus healing the servant (v. 51), showing Jesus' compassion towards his enemies. It is also a kindness to Peter, who would otherwise presumably have had to suffer the consequences of his violent act against an employee of the high priest. Jesus' mission was not to lead a rebellion (v. 52), and when the mob came with violence, Jesus refused to respond in kind. The result looks like weakness and defeat (v. 54).

Jesus explained, 'this is your hour – when darkness reigns' (v. 53). There are times in our lives – and in our world – when darkness reigns and violence wins, and it feels like our only option is to respond in violence too. Maybe you've experienced deep injustice or been trapped in a corner and wanted to lash out with words or gain vengeance through your position. Here, Jesus inspires us to a way of gentleness and non-violence, even when it looks like weakness, knowing that the hours of darkness do not have the final say.

Breathe in: When I am tempted to follow the violent ways of this world. Breathe out: Pour your Spirit of gentleness in me. Breathe in: When I am fearful or frustrated. Breathe out: Keep my focus on you.

TANYA MARLOW

Compassion for women who weep

A large number of people followed him, including women who mourned and wailed for him. Jesus turned and said to them, 'Daughters of Jerusalem, do not weep for me; weep for yourselves and for your children.' (Luke 23:27–28, NIV)

It is a rare person who can undergo extreme suffering and still think about others, but my friend Jenny Rowbory is like that. Constantly bed-bound and in pain with severe myalgic encephalomyelitis (ME), she is compassionate to her core and analyses any situation I'm going through with clarity and kindness.

Similarly, Jesus, weakened from beatings and walking towards death, sees a group of Jerusalem women who 'mourned and wailed for him' (Luke 23:27). Perhaps they were like professional mourners, or perhaps they were brave disciples, devoted to Christ. Either way, Jesus turns to them with compassion because of the coming destruction of Jerusalem at the hand of the Romans in AD70. Instead of crying for him, Jesus argues they will face a greater trauma, witnessing their children's suffering, and he wants to warn them of it (vv. 28–30). After all, using the metaphor of starting a fire, if the Romans are crucifying him now, 'when the tree is green', how much worse will it be for the Jews later on, 'when it is dry?' (v. 31). Jesus sees their compassion for his suffering and meets it with his compassion for theirs.

Jesus cared about women. John's account tells us that even on the cross, Jesus commissioned one of his dearest friends to look after his mother after his death, saying, 'Here is your mother' (John 19:27).

Women's pain is often overlooked by society today, as it was back then, but Jesus cares deeply about women, to the point that even at his death he was concerned about their welfare. If today you are tempted to dismiss your pain, come to Jesus, who says, 'weep for yourselves'. If you are tempted to dismiss your needs, come to Jesus, who oversaw the protection of his mother after his death.

When are you tempted to dismiss your own pain as a woman? In what way does Jesus' example encourage your boldness in prayer? In what way does Jesus' example inspire you to have compassion on others around you?

TANYA MARLOW

Hope at our lowest

My God, my God, why have you forsaken me? Why are you so far from saving me, so far from my cries of anguish?... But you, Lord, do not be far from me. You are my strength; come quickly to help me. (Psalm 22:1, 19, NIV)

What does 'lowliness' mean? We might think 'humility', which is certainly true. But the slightly unhappier side of lowliness is the 'low' part, and here we see Jesus at his very lowest. While we sometimes romanticise the cross, focusing on the theology, the reality is that Jesus was naked, exposed, hated and mocked, breathless, powerless and in pain. The cross declared him to be the bottom of society, the scum of the earth.

At that lowest of moments, Jesus cried: 'My God, my God, why have you forsaken me?' (Matthew 27:46). His cry of desperation perhaps echoes our cries when we too have felt powerless or confused, betrayed by others or in acute pain. Sometimes we cry out honestly to God: 'Why aren't you doing anything, God? Why have you just left me at my most vulnerable?' If you have ever felt like that, take comfort in knowing that even Jesus felt that way, too. While the sky literally went dark for Jesus (Matthew 27:45), it can feel dark for us physically and emotionally, and that in turn often affects our spiritual life.

However, even here, there is hope. Jesus' cry was a quote from Psalm 22, where we see the psalmist battling for faith between raw laments. The psalmist draws strength from what God has done before, 'In you our ancestors put their trust; they trusted and you delivered them' (Psalm 22:4). The psalm turns from a crisis of faith into prayer: 'Do not be far from me' (v. 11), and finally a declaration of trust: 'You are my strength; come quickly to help me' (v. 19). When you are at your lowest, lament, draw strength from God's actions in the past, and pray for God's help.

Jesus, thank you that we can come to you even at our lowest point because we know you have been there too. You know our pain. Please comfort us. Amen.

TANYA MARLOW

Humiliated and silenced

They stripped him and put a scarlet robe on him, and then twisted together a crown of thorns and set it on his head… They spat on him, and took the staff and struck him on the head again and again. (vv. 28–30, NIV)

I always think of Holy Saturday as a silent, empty day, between the sad drama of Good Friday and the joyful resurrection of Easter Sunday. Silence, when it's voluntarily taken, can be very freeing – a break from social media and the news cycle, perhaps. Likewise, humility can be releasing when we stop trying to prove ourselves and instead promote others.

However, I want to highlight an important distinction between being humble and being humiliated, and being silent versus being silenced, and for this we need to jump back a little in the narrative and look at Jesus' suffering.

Because it's just a few verses, we may miss its impact. First, Pilate 'had Jesus flogged' (v. 26), which is repeated pain, over and over, until you're at your breaking point and beyond. I often miss the detail that in the Praetorium (governor's residence) Jesus was surrounded not with a few mocking people but 'the whole company of soldiers round him' (v. 27), which could have been as many as 600 men. The scene is then set for his humiliation, where they dress him up, mock him as a pseudo-king, spit on him and beat him while he is defenceless (vv. 28–30). Whereas Jesus' silence before Pilate was a choice, here he has no chance to speak.

Whenever there is an imbalance of power and little choice at hand, this is abuse, and God does not wish this upon us. This is such an important distinction, perhaps especially for women, as we consider our place in the world. Too often Christian women stay in abusive relationships or workplaces because we believe we are being gentle and humble, rather than silenced and humiliated. Let's pray today for women around the world facing these situations.

Consider your various relationships. Where do you feel silenced? Where do you feel humiliated? Are you in danger of doing that to anyone else? Ask God for what you need: courage, rescue or perhaps wisdom.

TANYA MARLOW

The low raised up

'We are punished justly, for we are getting what our deeds deserve. But this man has done nothing wrong.' Then he said, 'Jesus, remember me when you come into your kingdom.' Jesus answered him, 'Truly I tell you, today you will be with me in paradise.' (vv. 41–43, NIV)

You may remember how awful it was to trip up and fall flat on your face when you were a child and running somewhere. Too winded, injured or indignant to do anything other than stay in place, I had to wait for a kind parent to scoop me up and carry me. I needed someone to raise me up and restore me.

In this short story, we see two people at their lowest who would be raised up. The first is Jesus. Jesus' last words are a quote from Psalm 31:5, 'Father, into your hands I commit my spirit' (v. 46), a prayer of trust from the midst of suffering. Today, on Easter Sunday, we remember that just three days later he was gloriously resurrected, having conquered sin and death once and for all. From the lowest point, he was raised to the highest, as Paul's poem puts it, 'Therefore God exalted him to the highest place and gave him the name that is above every name' (Philippians 2:9).

The second is the criminal, who recognises his wrong and Jesus' righteousness. At its most basic, that's all that saving faith is and all that is required of us. This simplest confession is rewarded with the greatest of promises: 'Today you will be with me in paradise' (v. 43).

When we are at our lowest or our most sinful or shamed, we too can look to Jesus and hear these words spoken as a promise to us and a guarantee of eternal life after death. Praise God – being low is never the end of the story, and our resurrected Jesus will always ultimately raise us up.

On this Easter Day, we praise you, Jesus, for making yourself low so we in turn could be raised up. Thank you for that promise of everlasting life with you in paradise. Hallelujah! Amen.

TANYA MARLOW

Gentle to the bruised

A bruised reed he will not break, and a smouldering wick he will not snuff out, till he has brought justice through to victory. In his name the nations will put their hope. (vv. 20–21, NIV)

Sadly, I am not great at keeping plants alive. Even spider plants, supposedly indestructible, seem to take one look at me and keel over. Once, though, I had an orange plant where the leaves started drooping and had ominous spots on them. I was about to give up on it, but a friend trimmed the right leaves, gave it the right food and it revived beautifully. I thought it was a hopeless case, but all it needed was a little love to thrive.

As we continue to explore Jesus, gentle and lowly, this week we are focusing on his time in ministry, watching Jesus' gentleness in action. Isaiah prophesied that God would provide a rescuer to reach out to the Gentiles: 'Here is my servant whom I have chosen… he will proclaim justice to the nations' (v. 18). Matthew sees Jesus as that promised servant. Although Jesus was trying to get away from the Pharisees who were plotting his death (v. 14), he was followed by a large crowd. Rather than dismiss the crowd for his own safety, Jesus showed compassion and 'healed all who were ill' (v. 15).

Jesus' gentle heart is described using the beautiful metaphors, 'A bruised reed he will not break, and a smouldering wick he will not snuff out' (v. 20). A bruised reed or smouldering wick, like my plant, look like hopeless cases, not worth bothering with. Isaiah was probably thinking of defeated small nations, but it also applies to any of us who feel bruised or hopeless.

Jesus is so gentle with a bruised reed that it will not break, and he is that way with us, too. Whether it's you personally, a friend or a nation that's bruised, turn to Jesus in prayer today, asking him to revive what looks to be hopeless.

Lord Jesus, as I consider this seemingly hopeless situation, I am tempted to despair. But you have compassion on those who are dismissed by others, the bruised, the wounded. Please revive this seemingly lost cause, I pray. Amen.

TANYA MARLOW

Gentle in healing

After he took him aside, away from the crowd, Jesus put his fingers into the man's ears. Then he spat and touched the man's tongue. (v. 33, NIV)

As a disabled person who has not been healed of my chronic illness, despite plenty of prayer, I know that reading the healing miracles can be difficult for many. As we read this account of Jesus healing a deaf man, I am conscious of the deaf community, who are often not only content with but proud of their deaf identity, and they have amazing close-knit communities that support them in their rich and silent life. Not everyone gets healing from illness, and not everyone needs healing from disability.

Having established that, what I love about this particular healing story is Jesus' understanding of the deaf man's situation as he heals him. If you look at Bible commentaries, there's a lot of theological head-scratching over why Jesus heals in such a convoluted way instead of just laying hands on him. If you ask someone who's had a cochlear implant to explain it, however, it's very clear. Jesus knew that going from a world of silence to a cacophony of noise would be overwhelming, so he takes the man 'aside, away from the crowd' (v. 33). Then Jesus explains to the man what's going to happen to him, not through words, but mime. First, he puts his fingers on the man's ears, then he spits to indicate healing (saliva was often used in those days as a kind of medicine) and touches his tongue (v. 33). Finally, he looks to heaven to show the man the healing is coming from God (v. 34).

Jesus' consideration of and gentleness towards this deaf man, meeting him in his unique situation, makes me love Jesus all the more. It also means that as Jesus heals us from emotional and spiritual wounds, he will do so gently, kindly, and in a way that is unique to us.

Lord Jesus, you heal, not like a brusque doctor or a showy performer, but a gentle friend. Meet me where I am today. Put balm on my soul where it is aching. Heal me with your gentleness, I pray. Amen.

TANYA MARLOW

Gentle in showing our faults

All the people saw this and began to mutter, 'He has gone to be the guest of a sinner.' But Zacchaeus stood up and said to the Lord, 'Look, Lord! Here and now I give half of my possessions to the poor.' (vv. 7–8, NIV)

In May 2012, Tim Challies, a popular American Christian speaker and blogger, reviewed a book written by Ann Voskamp, also a popular Christian speaker and blogger. The review was brutal, and a firestorm blew up on Twitter as followers of Voskamp squared up to Challies' supporters. Everyone waited to see what Ann's response would be to Tim, and when it came, it was extraordinary. She invited him to dinner – him and his family, to eat with her and her family, to get to know each other better. This simple act of her generous hospitality to Tim made him rethink the tone of his review, and he apologised.

This reminds me of Zacchaeus' story. Here was a 'chief tax collector' for the Romans, who was despised in Jewish society for colluding with the enemy, and 'was wealthy' from cheating people to make his own money on the side (vv. 2, 8). When Jesus saw him, he could have condemned him in front of the crowd and made an example of him. Instead, he invited himself over for dinner (v. 5). We're not told what they spoke about when Jesus met with him, only that Zacchaeus was a completely changed man afterwards, vowing to repay whomever he had cheated and giving half his money to the poor (v. 8). While others saw him as a traitor, Jesus simply saw him as 'lost' (v. 10).

This is the way of Jesus: not to loudly condemn us or frighten us into repentance. When we have communion with Jesus, through prayer and in church, Jesus' gentle Spirit makes us gradually aware of what needs to be different and then works in us to make those changes. So today, just focus on enjoying Jesus' company. Amazing things can happen when we do.

How do you feel about the image of eating with Jesus, and that changing our hearts? Is there anyone in your life who needs your hospitality rather than your condemnation?

TANYA MARLOW

Gentle to the weary

'Come to me, all you who are weary and burdened, and I will give you rest. Take my yoke upon you and learn from me, for I am gentle and humble in heart, and you will find rest for your souls.' (vv. 28–29, NIV)

As I write this, I feel weariness on many levels. Just recovering from a nasty virus, I am physically tired. As a parent, I find the grey skies and relentless routine of the school days monotonous, and I am worn down by the news cycle which makes me feel powerless and angry and scared all at the same time.

I know that some of you reading this will be wearied by your body, which refuses to do anything without complaining or collapsing, or your mind, which keeps travelling to negative and destructive thoughts. Some of you will be exhausted by the challenges of being a parent, either physically or emotionally. Others will be overwhelmed by financial worries, or job instability, or hostility from family, or bullying from colleagues, or the distance from ageing parents as they become more vulnerable. Some will be weary from loneliness.

All of us need to hear these beautiful words from Jesus once more and to come to him in our weariness and with our burdens. 'I will give you rest', he promises us. Jesus invites us to: 'Take my yoke upon you… For my yoke is easy and my burden is light' (vv. 29–30). The image is of two animals, plough horses perhaps, who are yoked together and pulling the plough behind them. In this image, our yoke is not completely removed, but instead we walk with Jesus. As we do we find that the 'burden is light', because Jesus takes the weight of it all as we move alongside him.

He invites us: 'Learn from me, for I am gentle and humble in heart' (v. 29). As we've been exploring these studies, we have seen the beauty of Jesus' gentle leadership. This is the God we walk alongside. Today, learn from Jesus and take his yoke.

Jesus, gentle and humble, I come to you today. I want to learn from you. I need your rest in my weariness. Today, I take your easy yoke upon my shoulders and walk alongside you. Amen.

TANYA MARLOW

Two pictures of humility

'I tell you that this man, rather than the other, went home justified before God. For all those who exalt themselves will be humbled, and those who humble themselves will be exalted.' (v. 14, NIV)

Take a moment to consider who most annoys you. Maybe it's someone in your family who rubs you up the wrong way, perhaps a work colleague or church member who is always interrupting you, or maybe more generally it's people who disagree with you theologically or politically. Whoever that is, I've got uncomfortable news for you: that's your equivalent of the Pharisee saying to himself, 'God, I thank you that I am not like…' (v. 11).

To respond to the call to be humble in this world – in other words, to know our right place in this world alongside others and under the rule of God – we start with our thought-life. It can be really tempting, especially in our increasingly polarised society, to identify only with the people like us and make pantomime villains of the ones we dislike. We may think it's fair enough to compare ourselves favourably against evil leaders, and there is certainly a place for justice-seeking, protest and accountability. But the Pharisee in the parable was smug that he was not like 'evildoers' (v. 11), so that should give us pause. To be humble means remembering that we are all human and sinners, all in need of God's mercy (v. 13).

We have two pictures of humility here: the tax collector who is honest about his shortcomings, and the innocent children coming to Jesus with nothing to give but themselves yet receiving the kingdom of God as a gift (v. 17). For those of us struggling with smugness today, we can learn from the tax collector. But for those of us struggling to know our worth, we can take encouragement from the joyful humility that little children have, trusting in the God who loves us.

What posture of humility is God calling you to take this morning: looking inwards and confessing your shortcomings like the tax collector, or looking upwards at Jesus like a child?

TANYA MARLOW

Blessed are the gentle

He said: 'Blessed are the poor in spirit, for theirs is the kingdom of heaven. Blessed are those who mourn, for they will be comforted. Blessed are the meek, for they will inherit the earth.' (vv. 2–5, NIV)

Two weeks ago, we began this series by thinking about how our world rewards the powerful, the violent, the arrogant and those who exalt themselves and put others down. Jesus, however, shows us a way of gentleness and lowliness.

As we have studied the scriptures, we have seen Jesus the lowly, who was fully God, yet fully human and vulnerable, needing assistance from others and help from God the Father as he wrestled with suffering. We have also seen Jesus as powerful but gentle, encountering individuals and lovingly meeting their unique needs for healing, lament, change or refreshment. We have also been reminded that Jesus, who made himself low, has been exalted to the highest place, gloriously resurrected so that we too can be raised up in eternal life with him.

Today, we're looking at Jesus' words in the sermon on the mount. He blesses people not welcomed or valued by the world: 'the poor in spirit… those who mourn… the peacemakers… those who are persecuted…' (vv. 1–10). One of the groups listed is 'the meek' (v. 5). The word 'meek' here is better translated as gentle, as it is the same root in Greek as Matthew 11:29 ('for I am gentle and humble in heart') and Matthew 21:5 ('gentle and riding on a donkey'). Even if the world doesn't reward us, we are called to be gentle, and God will bless us for it.

Blessed are the lowly, for one day they will be exalted. Blessed are the gentle, for one day they will 'inherit the earth' (v. 5). As we leave this series, my hope is that we're inspired to live counterculturally, not to strive to a form of success that exploits others, but to look up to God in our lowness and vulnerability, and live gently, like Jesus.

As you review the past two weeks, what have you most loved about Jesus' gentle and lowly leadership? What do you need to receive from Jesus? How has this series changed how you want to be in this world?

TANYA MARLOW

God stepped in

Sandra Wheatley writes...

This coming week we shall read familiar Old Testament stories of people who encountered God in amazing ways as he stepped into their often messy and challenging lives, and into the very demanding and difficult situations they faced.

They had a close encounter of the divine kind – an intervention often defined as an extraordinary act of God that interrupts the natural course of events we face, overriding our human efforts or limitations, and bringing supernatural solutions to impossible situations.

In Old Testament pre-incarnation times, encounters with God were rare and known as a 'theophany'. We have the benefit of a personal relationship with Emmanuel – 'God-with-us-with-skin-and-bones' as a little friend of mine once said – but nevertheless there is much we can learn from the lives of these familiar people.

I pray that not only will we be able to identify in some way with their stories and experiences – their messed-up lives, damaged relationships and their attempts to put right what had gone wrong – but also that, as we explore how God stepped into their lives, we will recognise how God steps into our lives too and be assured of that wonderful truth that nothing ever can or will separate us from God (Romans 8:35–39).

I can testify that when I have found myself teetering on the edge of some self-made crisis, or have experienced hurt and misunderstanding from those around me, I have seen and experienced God stepping in. When the diagnosis of multiple sclerosis came and the whole axis of my life seemed to shift, God stepped in.

When the loss of all I had worked and aimed for lay in tatters at my feet as I literally couldn't walk or work anymore, God stepped in. I'm sure many of you will have had similar experiences.

It is a delight to be with you as we read again the stories of Hagar, who saw the God who saw her; of Hannah whose anguished prayer was heard; of Moses whose incredible theophany would determine the history of Israel; and other biblical characters in need of God stepping in and transforming their seemingly forgotten, abandoned, abused or overlooked lives.

What God did then, he is still doing now. He still sees, hears and knows each of us. He bends low to hear our whispered prayer (Psalm 116:1–2, NLT).

God knows our circumstances

The angel of the Lord found Hagar near a spring in the desert; it was the spring that is beside the road to Shur. (v. 7, NIV)

Along a desert road, beside a remote, unnamed well, the angel of the Lord approached a pregnant, abused, runaway slave named Hagar.

How she came to be there is told in this chapter of Genesis. Hagar was the young Egyptian servant of Sarai, the wife of Abram, and may well have been taken from Egypt by Sarai and Abram when they left (Genesis 12:10–20).

As her story unfolds, we see the mess often caused when those given a promise by God (Genesis 15:5) that is seemingly not happening take matters into their own hands.

Sarai concocts a plan whereby she can have a family despite, at that time, being infertile. She 'gave' Hagar to her husband 'to be his wife' (v. 3). He complied and Hagar conceived. When Hagar realised she was pregnant, she began to act as if she had the upper hand over Sarai and began to despise her. Sarai responded by mistreating Hagar to the point that Hagar fled into the wilderness.

We might think that Hagar's attitude towards Sarai contributed to her circumstances, but nonetheless God stepped in and met with her when she was exhausted and despairing by a desert pool. He called her by her name and asked her where she had come from and where she was going. He listened to her reply and then told her to go back to her mistress. But God also gave her an incredible promise about her unborn son, whose name, Ishmael, would mean, 'God hears'.

As God stepped in, Hagar realised he was the God who 'sees' – not only right *where* she was but also exactly *how* she was. She became the first person to name God 'El Roi': 'I have seen the One who sees me' (v. 13). Wonderful. May you know, as Hagar did, that God sees you too.

Read Romans 8:28 and let the truth of it be his gift to you today. May you sense God hearing your cry and stepping in to your circumstances.

SANDRA WHEATLEY

God meets us where we are

There the angel of the Lord appeared to [Moses] in flames of fire from within a bush. (v. 2, NIV)

Moses' life was anything but ordinary, and yet here he is in a desert, tending his father-in-law's sheep. His early life is recorded in Exodus 2, which explains the reason why this former prince was living in very different circumstances. Everything had changed. Now he's a nobody, doing nothing very significant, in the middle of nowhere. However, God had a plan, and that plan included Moses and a remarkable 'stepping in'.

In the desert where Moses tended sheep, burning bushes were a regular occurrence – in the heat of the day, tinder-dry bushes easily ignited. Except this one got Moses' attention, this one didn't burn up, and this one spoke and knew Moses' name! This became the place that God stepped in, and from that moment of encountering God, Moses' life would be radically transformed. He would supervise the Israelites' escape from Egypt and lead them to the promised land.

Burning bushes aren't very common in north Northumberland, where I live, but I believe that wherever we find ourselves – physically, emotionally or geographically – God can find us.

I remember one summer day years ago when I was reading this story. It was one of those days when the routine of daily living with disability and intractable pain made me feel as if God was done with me and there was little else for me to do. I glanced across my garden. The trees and bushes were still, nothing moved. I began to wonder if God still used bushes to make himself known. Just then a small bush moved gently, then stopped. I said, 'Was that you, God?' and the bush gently moved again. I leaned back on my bed and waved back at the bush that had 'waved' to me. God had stepped in to my day.

Father God, meet us in our ordinary days; draw us to you in extraordinary ways and may we then be ablaze for you. Amen.

SANDRA WHEATLEY

God sees our potential

The angel of the Lord came and sat down under the oak in Ophrah that belonged to Joash the Abiezrite, where his son Gideon was threshing wheat in a winepress to keep it from the Midianites. (v. 11, NIV)

Israel was again in a mess of its own doing (v. 1). Oppressed and living in fear of the Midianites and Amalekites, the people cried out to the Lord. They were left in no doubt that God was not best pleased with them (vv. 7–10). Nevertheless, God in his mercy stepped in and chose the unlikeliest of people to fulfil his purpose.

Gideon, our unlikely hero, was very much out of place threshing wheat in a winepress, scared of being found by the marauding Midianites. Yet it's here the angel of the Lord found him.

He called Gideon 'a mighty warrior'. Gideon responded with a number of questions, including how someone as weak and timid as him, from the weakest family and of the smallest tribe in Israel could be chosen to deliver Israel (v. 15)? But God saw in Gideon what Gideon couldn't, and into a life paralysed by fear, doubt and questioning, God stepped in.

I love this story. I can identify with Gideon's timidity, his bewilderment at his encounter with God, his need for reassurance, and his awareness of himself as not being good enough, strong enough or clever enough to be considered a 'mighty warrior'.

Perhaps you do too. We often see those around us as being more gifted, more confident and more able. Surely those are the people God would choose to use, but that isn't how God works, even if at times we do! 1 Corinthians 1:27–29 blows that out of the water.

The story of Gideon is a reminder to those of us who feel overlooked, downtrodden or not quite good or able enough that God steps in.

Remind us, Lord, of our value and worth to you, that Jesus died for us to prove that to be true. 'Who, me?' we ask. 'Yes, you' is your reply!

SANDRA WHEATLEY

God hears our heartache

Because the Lord had closed Hannah's womb, her rival kept provoking her in order to irritate her. This went on year after year. Whenever Hannah went up to the house of the Lord, her rival provoked her till she wept and would not eat. (vv. 6–7, NIV).

Another story of two women and one man. Again, one woman can conceive and have children, the other can't. The stigma of infertility in biblical times was immense, but Hannah also had to endure Peninnah's constant taunts.

Every year, Elkanah, Peninnah, her entourage of children and Hannah went to Shiloh to worship and sacrifice at the tabernacle. The same journey, the same sacrificial meal, the same taunts and provocation from Peninnah and the same lack of understanding from Elkanah (v. 8).

Hannah never retaliated; she was true to her name, which means 'grace', but one year, her desperation, sadness and longing for a child got the better of her.

This time she 'stood up' (v. 9). I wonder if it was in that moment that God stepped in.

Her silent prayer came from the depths of her being. It was the kind of prayer perhaps we too have prayed at some point in our lives – not a pretty prayer, not neat and measured, but honest, messy, as words and tears intermingled. Hannah poured out her heart to God, and God stepped in.

This pivotal moment for Hannah was to change not only her life, but also the course of history for the people of Israel, as the son God gave her would become the prophet Samuel. His name means 'God has heard'. What an incredible outcome from the cries of a desperate women.

I have no way of knowing the circumstances you are facing or the years and years you have endured in silence, longing for God to see, to hear… to step in.

As I'm writing this, I'll pause and pray for you as you pray your very own 'Hannah-prayer' if you need to.

Father God, you know our story. Hear our prayer. Amen.

SANDRA WHEATLEY

God knows our need

Elijah was afraid and ran for his life… He came to a broom bush, sat down under it and prayed that he might die. 'I have had enough, Lord,' he said. 'Take my life.' (vv. 3–4, NIV)

Elijah was a mighty and powerful prophet – the previous chapters of 1 Kings reveal a life lived at a breakneck speed. 1 Kings 18 tells how he had defeated the 450 prophets of Baal and then commanded that they be slaughtered, resulting in King Ahab's wife, Jezebel, threatening to kill him. So, Elijah ran, literally for his life. He ran for an entire day, then collapsed under a broom tree and implored God to take his life!

'I have had enough, Lord.' Does Elijah's story resonate with you today? Are you exhausted by circumstances, running on empty, seeking an escape and any shelter you can find?

Exhausted by his journey, Elijah fell asleep. Then God stepped in, not to kill him, but to prepare a simple meal of baked bread and water. With a gentle touch Elijah is woken and encouraged to eat. He falls asleep again. Then he's gently woken again and given words of encouragement that nourish his soul: 'Get up and eat, for the journey is too much for you' (v. 7). God knew exactly where he was, how he was and what he needed.

Years ago, when I'd fled to my 'broom tree', utterly spent and exhausted by circumstance and illness, I too asked God to take my life, because I'd had enough. God stepped in, using many guises. He ensured I was rested and nourished and could face the journey ahead, with him.

I emerged with the words of a hymn resonating in my heart and soul: 'Take my life and let it be, consecrated Lord to thee.' The words 'Take my life' now had a different meaning and came from a heart of gratitude at having met with God.

Make the words of the hymn your prayer today, and pray for anyone you know who is struggling, that they may encounter God afresh today.

SANDRA WHEATLEY

God's love has no limit

And when [Manasseh] prayed to him, the Lord was moved by his entreaty and listened to his plea. (v. 13, NIV)

Manasseh was the son of Hezekiah, whom God had granted another 15 years of life (2 Kings 20:1–6), during which time Manasseh was born. He started to reign when he was twelve years old and ruled for 55 years. He was not a good king, and 2 Kings 21:16 sums up his reign as being marked by bloodshed, idolatry and leading his people astray. By any human measure, he had gone far beyond the point of return.

Throughout history, there have been countless lives lived as Manasseh did, rulers whose actions parallel the cruelty and destruction of Manasseh's reign. The difference however – as far as we know – is that Manasseh is the only king or ruler who prayed and humbled himself before the God of his fathers. The account of his reign in 2 Chronicles 33 describes a complete turnaround in his life as God stepped in. Taken as a prisoner to Babylon and in great distress, Manasseh turned to God, and God heard his prayer (v. 13). Grace, mercy and forgiveness flooded into Manasseh's life. He was released and returned to Jerusalem, and spent the rest of his life putting right the wrongs he had committed.

This story shows us that no one is beyond God's reach. God's 'no limits' nature doesn't mean he overlooks evil or cancels justice. Manasseh still endured exile and humiliation. But even in judgement, God's mercy reached him. Society may write people off – and we often do – but God's reach extends beyond our thresholds of possibility. His grace, mercy and forgiveness are available to everyone who turns to him. How might that encourage our prayers both for ourselves and for world events and leaders today?

Thank you, Lord, that our best days don't define us and neither do our worst. You define, forgive and restore us. Amen.

SANDRA WHEATLEY

God is with us

'If we are thrown into the blazing furnace, the God we serve is able to deliver us from it, and he will deliver us from Your Majesty's hand. But even if he does not, we want you to know, Your Majesty, that we will not serve your gods.' (vv. 17–18, NIV)

Daniel, Shadrach, Meshach and Abednego were taken into captivity in Babylon (Daniel 1:3–7) to be trained and then to enter the King of Babylon's service. They had proved themselves excellent workers, but their unwillingness to compromise their loyalty to God meant they were facing certain death as they were brought before King Nebuchadnezzar for disobeying his edict (v. 12).

Shadrach, Meshach and Abednego stood firm before an angry king and a blazing furnace. They proclaimed their faith in God, but it is the next sentence that resonates deeply with me: 'But even if he does not…'

This is something I have also said in the midst of some hard and harsh times, trusting with all my heart in the promises of God, but adding through gritted teeth, 'But even if he does not, I'll still trust him!'

When Shadrach, Meshach and Abednego are thrown into the furnace, we learn that there is someone with them (v. 25). This is a story not about a God who is distantly watching on, but one who steps into the furnace with them. The three men survived without being burned, singed or even smelling of the smoke of the furnace.

There is a wonderful promise from God in Isaiah 43:2 – whatever circumstance we are dealing with, whether our faith is under fire or under a deluge that overwhelms us, God has promised to be with us. He will step in.

We can trust that whatever trial or challenge we face or are facing, we will have our very own close encounter of the divine kind at God's appointed time and in unexpected ways.

Father God, whatever we face today, may we know you're with us. Amen.

SANDRA WHEATLEY

The letter to the Galatians

Georgie Tennant writes...

The letter from Paul to the Galatians is a fascinating insight into some of the struggles faced by the emerging church. Paul, formerly Saul, had lived his whole his life under the rigour of strict religious traditions. Then, on the road to Damascus, a dramatic encounter with God transformed him from zealous persecutor of Christians to passionate preacher of the grace available to all through the risen Christ (Acts 9).

This message is at the heart of the letter to the Galatians. Paul, writing from Ephesus, has heard news from Galatia that has frustrated and bewildered him: some of the Jewish Christians there have been insisting that anyone receiving Christ and becoming part of the early church must conform to Jewish religious traditions. What's more, he has also heard that Peter, a chief apostle and church leader, has stopped eating with the Gentile Christians, fearing the reaction of a group of Jewish believers visiting from Jerusalem. Paul is outraged by his hypocrisy, fearing the damage it would cause to the new and fledgling faith of the Gentiles.

For the whole of this letter, Paul goes to great pains to clarify the gospel message: Christ died for everyone, and the only way to walk in the freedom of forgiveness and reconciliation to God is by faith and nothing else. We can't add to it by outward works – if we did it wouldn't be a gospel at all! No outward behaviour can change the facts: Christ died for us, and we are accepted and forgiven through faith alone.

We might join Paul in wondering how Peter had become so hypocritical, but we might sympathise too. Isn't it easy to worry that faith alone is not enough – to want to perform in such a way that we feel more deserving of our salvation? In the days that follow, we will look together at some of the things that cause us to stray into 'gospel plus,' territory. What do we try to add in or leave out? How can we avoid falling into the same traps as those early Christians?

Join me over the next twelve days as we journey through the book of Galatians. I hope you will come to this familiar text with fresh eyes, and I pray that, as you do, God will ignite a renewed passion and excitement in your heart for his incredible gift of outrageous grace.

No other gospel

I am astonished that you are so quickly deserting the one who called you to live in the grace of Christ and are turning to a different gospel – which is really no gospel at all. (vv. 6–7, NIV)

Paul's letters to the churches in the New Testament usually start out communicating grace, peace and encouragement. After his archetypal introduction here in Galatians, Paul dives straight in, using strong language to make the point he is so passionate about: the gospel is the gospel and must not be added to or detracted from.

It must have been a difficult letter to receive. Isn't it often the case that, when we stray from the truth of the gospel, it isn't because we are doing it deliberately, but because small, subtle adjustments creep in? It is hard to take a reality check, let go of those things and start afresh.

But that is exactly what Paul is urging the Galatian churches to do: to recognise any attitudes or behaviours that are not in keeping with the true gospel of grace. To throw out anything they have inadvertently or deliberately added to their definition of a follower of Christ and walk again in the freedom of grace.

Two thousand years later, this message is still sorely needed. Personally, I know I sometimes convince myself that if only I read my Bible more, prayed longer and attended more church events, God would be pleased with me. If I was kinder to my colleagues and my teenagers and didn't get cross in traffic, perhaps God would look upon me more favourably. How could he love a messy sinner like me, without reservation?

But that is the great news of this letter. The message of the gospel is a message of grace right in the middle of the messy reality of my everyday life and yours. There is nothing we can do to earn it. He has given it to us in Christ, and we simply receive it though faith.

Take some time today to reflect on whether you are inadvertently adding to the gospel of grace. Ask God for his help to understand which areas of your life need a fresh revelation of his astonishing grace.

GEORGIE TENNANT

Your unique mission

I had been entrusted with the task of preaching the gospel to the uncircumcised, just as Peter had been to the circumcised. For God, who was at work in Peter as an apostle to the circumcised, was also at work in me as an apostle to the Gentiles. (vv. 7–8, NIV)

In this part of his letter, Paul takes time to explain his credentials. He wants to ensure that those receiving his words are convinced that his doctrine is sound. He describes his time with other church leaders in Jerusalem, where he sought (and gained) confirmation that he was preaching the gospel accurately and without heresy to the Gentiles.

Paul goes on to acknowledge the difference between his calling and Peter's – his to the Gentiles and Peter's to the Jews, each man uniquely equipped to carry the gospel to different people and places.

This is an area where we can easily find ourselves adding to the gospel: the mistaken belief that people called to a particular type of ministry or service are 'more Christian' than others. It is so easy to look at preachers, evangelists and missionaries and feel that my calling or gifting is inferior and earns me less kudos in God's eyes. Wrong!

I love the work of the London Institute of Contemporary Christianity, whose mission it is to encourage all Christians, whoever and wherever they are, to spread the good news of Christ on their own 'front lines'. It is a great leveller. The teacher, the charity worker, the retired person extending hospitality to their neighbour, the new mum at a toddler group, the baker, the taxi driver – each of us are uniquely placed and anointed to carry the gift of grace to the places we go and the people around us.

How do we do that? Not from a place of trying to perform our way into God's 'good books', but from our position as recipients of God's grace, who have good news we can't help but communicate.

Take time today to thank God for his incredible gift of grace. Think about what you might consider your 'front line', and pray about how you can carry God's gift of grace to it this week.

GEORGIE TENNANT

Christ in you

For before certain men came from James, [Peter] used to eat with the Gentiles. But when they arrived, he began to draw back and separate himself from the Gentiles because he was afraid of those who belonged to the circumcision group. (v. 12, NIV)

It might sound silly, but when I read the New Testament letters, I sometimes forget that the pioneers of early Christianity are the same men we read about in the gospels. They feel like different characters as the story moves forward, but they are the very same men who walked with Jesus and learned from him. We sometimes mistakenly view them as somehow superhuman and infallible, but they weren't. Even they made mistakes – as Peter does in the passage we are reading today.

We can perhaps relate to Peter. In the gospels he often acted rashly, sometimes earning Jesus' rebuke, but always being restored to him in love and grace. When he was filled with the Holy Spirit, he changed and grew, becoming a fearless preacher of the gospel and writer of letters that still speak to us today. However, here we see Paul admonishing him for behaving hypocritically. Peter was a Jew, freed from the restrictions of Jewish customs through his faith in Jesus. He had been eating with Gentile believers, united in Christ, not by external rituals; but now, fearing the visiting Jews from Jerusalem, he had drawn back. Like all of us, Peter continued to be a work in progress, needing patience and grace.

Paul reminds both Peter and the Galatians that, 'if righteousness could be gained through the law, Christ died for nothing!' (v. 21). We need to be reminded of this too. If you are striving, today, to reach a particular standard or perform in a particular way, lean into the truth afresh that it is Christ in you, not your efforts, standards or behaviour, that changes lives deeply (yours and those around you), now and for all eternity. And when you feel like you're getting it all wrong – there is grace!

Thank God, today, that it is only through Christ that we have grace for today and the assurance of eternity with him. Put some worship music on, lay down your own efforts and rest in his loving arms.

GEORGIE TENNANT

Faith or good behaviour?

Are you so foolish? After beginning by means of the Spirit, are you now trying to finish by means of the flesh? (v. 3, NIV)

Have you ever tried to create a delicious meal or cake only for it all to go horribly wrong? I have a chocolate fudge cake recipe that never fails, but when I tried to make it for a friend, it came out of the oven flat, rubbery and inedible. At first, I couldn't work out why, but I later realised I had put in plain (all-purpose) flour instead of self-raising. I had deviated from the recipe, accidentally and only slightly, but with disastrous results.

On a much deeper level, this is what Paul is trying to prevent in the Galatian church. People were adding little ingredients of their own to the gospel, and Paul could foresee this having far-reaching and disastrous results.

As we reach this part of Paul's letter, he is very much warming to this theme. He uses strong language, calling them 'foolish' and 'bewitched' (v. 1), displaying his intense frustration that they have fallen away from the true gospel. He prompts them to reflect on where their faith began – with the Holy Spirit touching their lives, calling them to faith, changing them from the inside out. He challenges them to appraise themselves honestly and notice where they are trying to take over from the Spirit's work, making it about them and their 'works' instead.

It is something we must continually reflect on too, as it is an easy trap to fall into. As Paul wrote in one of his later letters, 'He who began a good work in you will carry it on to completion until the day of Christ Jesus' (Philippians 1:6). Here is the key – Christ in us does the work, not we, ourselves, through our own strength or efforts. Only through Christ can we truly live our lives as God intended us to.

What are you doing today that started in the Spirit, but is continuing through your own efforts? Give it back to God in prayer today, asking him to refill it with his presence and power.

GEORGIE TENNANT

Clothing ourselves

So in Christ Jesus you are all children of God through faith, for all of you who were baptised into Christ have clothed yourselves with Christ. (vv. 26–27, NIV)

Last year, my son was in a wonderful production of *The Sound of Music*, with a local amateur dramatics' society. He played the part of Kurt Von Trapp, the youngest of the two boys in the Von Trapp family. Yes, I was that over-eager parent who went to watch the show twice!

One of the great turning points in the months of practice was the day the costumes arrived. As they began to rehearse in costume instead of in their own clothes, a transformation began to occur. He was no longer a 21st century teenager; he was now a convincing child of the 1940s. By the time the opening night of the show arrived, it was no longer my son on the stage. He was truly in role, Kurt Von Trapp, convincing in every way. His outfits didn't just clothe him – they transformed him into someone entirely different.

This is the metaphor Paul gives us in this part of his letter. He reminds the Galatians that, 'all of you who were baptised into Christ have clothed yourselves with Christ' (v. 27). The NLT puts it this way: 'all who have been united with Christ in baptism have put on Christ, like putting on new clothes.' These aren't awkward, gaping clothes belonging to someone else, like when David tried to wear Saul's armour. These are custom made, especially for us. They fit perfectly. They transform us into someone completely different – someone set free to live assured of our adoption as a child of God, through Christ's sacrifice.

Thank God that he doesn't leave us naked and ashamed, but transforms us, as we put on the clothing he has provided. Are you wearing the right clothing today? Let it transform you from the inside out.

Spend some time today thanking God for clothing you with Christ. Ask him to let his clothing transform you, ever more deeply, as you wear it each day.

GEORGIE TENNANT

Children or slaves?

So you are no longer a slave, but God's child; and since you are his child, God has made you also an heir. (v. 7, NIV)

In yesterday's passage, Paul introduced the metaphor of sonship versus slavery. There, he expounded that the law was a guardian, taking care of us as well as it could until Christ came, enabling us to be adopted as God's sons (remembering, of course, that the gendered language of Paul's culture doesn't exclude women – we too are adopted as God's children). In today's passage, Paul deepens that metaphor with the image of our transformation from slaves to sons.

Let's dwell for a moment on what that means. Slavery, though tragically still existing in many forms, is mercifully alien to most of us. It takes some imagination to remind ourselves of the vastly different positions of son and slave. A son had access to all that was his father's. Slaves had no rights; they were property. They had to do back-breaking work in horrendous conditions for little reward. Only if someone came and paid a price for their freedom could they be 'redeemed' and walk away to freedom. Otherwise, they were trapped in a life they hadn't chosen. Some were even born into these unfortunate circumstances.

We didn't choose to be born into captivity either, but we were – captivity to sin due to the fall. God the Father's hopes and promises for us couldn't be fulfilled while we were slaves to the sin of the fallen world into which we were born. We couldn't inherit anything from God, as a Father, in that state. But Jesus changed everything. Only he could pay the price for our freedom so that we could live as God's children, as originally intended. Not as slaves, with no relationship with him and no hope for the future, but as beloved sons and daughters, heirs to all of his promises. This is something to celebrate!

This is a hard concept to grasp. Ask the Holy Spirit today to give you a fresh and deep understanding of everything it means to be a child of God – forgiven, accepted, free.

GEORGIE TENNANT

An uncomfortable gift

But now that you know God – or rather are known by God – how is it that you are turning back to those weak and miserable forces? Do you wish to be enslaved by them all over again? (v. 9 NIV)

Isn't it frustrating when you see someone you love making damaging choices and not heeding advice that might improve things for them? As parents, particularly, if you have 'been there and done that', with an undesirable outcome, you might go to great pains to convince your children not to make the same mistakes as you.

This is the tone Paul adopts here – a loving but frustrated parent, trying to explain with great urgency why the Galatians should avoid going down the route he sees them taking. Paul has been set free from the very thing he fears the Galatians are pursuing – religion rather than a grace-filled relationship with Christ. Paul was the most zealous of all zealots. He would have adhered strictly to every Jewish law and custom and berated those who didn't. He knew what it was like to be captive to that and then set free into grace, and he doesn't want the Galatians to find themselves where he was. He has experienced freedom in Christ and wants to jealously guard it for others.

Paul is essentially asking the Galatians why they would go back to a counterfeit when they have experienced the real thing? We need to ask ourselves the same question. We live in such a performance-oriented culture, it is a hard thing to lay down. It perhaps feels easier, more natural, to have something measurable to live up to; it is more comfortable to earn something than be given it for free.

It is a belief easily slipped into and therefore something we must keep returning to and challenging. Living by grace and not by works doesn't come naturally to us. We have to perform in so many areas of life – but not this one. Let's keep reminding ourselves of that with deep gratitude.

Spend some time today in prayer, asking God to reveal any areas of your life where you are trying to earn his love and approval. Lay them down and thank him that he gives it to you for free.

GEORGIE TENNANT

Our way or God's?

His son by the slave woman was born according to the flesh, but his son by the free woman was born as the result of a divine promise. (v. 23, NIV)

When our second son was small, 'My can do it myself!' was a phrase we heard regularly. There were times when we encouraged his independence, but there were many occasions when things would have gone more smoothly if he had stopped trying to do it his way and trusted that we had skills and abilities that exceeded his. He didn't need to struggle on his own.

In this part of his letter, Paul mentions an Old Testament incident where a similar thing happened – Abram and Sarai, instead of trusting the promise of their heavenly Father, took things into their own hands, with disastrous results. Abram, old and childless, with a wife unable to conceive, had been promised by God that he would have an heir. Time passed and, seeing no evidence of the promise's fulfilment, he and Sarai plotted to solve the problem. Sarai suggested Abram sleep with Hagar, her maid. The result was indeed a son – but not the one he had been promised. Isaac came later, but the damage was already done. Jealousy, hatred and conflict followed for the children and their descendants.

Paul reminds the Galatians that 'at that time the son born according to the flesh persecuted the son born by the power of the Spirit' (rendered by *The Message* as: 'the child who came from faithless plotting... harassed the child who came... from the faithful promise'). Then he delivers a hard-to-digest comparison: 'It is the same now' (v. 29). He challenges the Galatians not to make the same mistake of making a mockery of God's promises by taking things into their own hands.

We must heed the challenge too. Rather than taking things into our own hands, let's instead practise relaxing into the arms of a loving Father, who has already taken care of it all.

Spend time today reflecting and praying: are there things you are wrestling out of God's capable hands into your less capable ones? Are you willing to re-surrender them back to him today?

GEORGIE TENNANT

Who cut in on you?

You were running a good race. Who cut in on you to keep you from obeying the truth? (v. 7, NIV)

Have you ever watched the cycling event called the keirin? In it, cyclists are led out by a motorised 'derny' bike. They stay behind it for four of the eight laps of the race, one behind the other, in their own space. Halfway around lap five, the derny exits the track and the fun begins: the cyclists bundle together, each pushing hard to cross the finish line first. Sometimes, one cuts in on another, causing both of them to spin up the sides of the velodrome and crash out of the race.

The race metaphor Paul uses in today's passage resonates with me. So often I have been 'running my race' well and something cuts in and sends me tripping and stumbling off the track I heard an excellent sermon that has stuck with me, based on Hebrews 12:1: 'Let us throw off everything that hinders and the sin that so easily entangles. And let us run with perseverance the race marked out for us.' The preacher challenged us to identify our own 'so easilies' – the things that cut in and trip us up. Paul makes the same challenge, asking the Galatians what it is that has cut in on the race they were running.

For them, it was persuasive false teaching. For me it has been small things (busyness, overwhelm, fear of others' opinions) and enormous ones (the loss of a baby and, later, my sister). Circumstances and experiences have raised doubts in my mind about God's character, provision and promises. How have I dealt with those and continued to run? I go back to central, eternal truths that underpin everything: God is good, and he loves me. Without those, the waves crash, and I am wiped out. With them, I can withstand anything.

Reflect today on the 'so easilies' that cut in on you regularly, tripping you up and sending you spinning. Write down some truths about God and his character to cling on to each time they try to cut in on you.

GEORGIE TENNANT

Free to bear fruit

Since we live by the Spirit, let us keep in step with the Spirit. (v. 25, NIV)

Have you heard the old children's song about the fruit of the Spirit? The song tells us that coconuts, bananas, melons and other fruits are not fruit of the Spirit, then goes on to list the ones that do qualify: love, joy, peace, patience, kindness, goodness, faithfulness, gentleness and self-control. I challenge you to listen to the song, then read the list back over without singing it! It's a real 'ear worm'.

Why does it seem as if Paul is shifting towards talking about outward expressions of faith here, when he has previously gone to such great pains to point out that performance is not what the gospel is all about? The truth is that he isn't. His point is that, as Christians, we behave in new ways not to earn our freedom, but because we are free already, in Christ. Our freedom will lead to good fruit, not the other way round.

Is it the right way round in your life? Are you trying to be loving, kind, patient and gentle in the hope that it will give you more chance of being considered a good Christian, by God and others? Or is the fruit growing in your life because of what the Holy Spirit is doing within?

It's crucial to get it the right way round, so we don't become bound up in the same performance mentality that Paul was challenging in the Galatians. Of course, we want to avoid the list of sins and display the list of fruit – and we will if we are living 'freely, animated and motivated by God's Spirit' (v. 18, MSG). But keep remembering that when it goes wrong, as it will, because we are human, there's grace all over again – time and time and time again.

Thank God for the grace he has poured out on you that enables you to live 'animated and motivated' by his Holy Spirit. Ask him to help you grow more of his fruit in your life.

GEORGIE TENNANT

A chocolate chip on my chin

Brothers and sisters, if someone is caught in a sin, you who live by the Spirit should restore that person gently. But watch yourselves, or you also may be tempted. (v. 1, NIV)

As a new teacher, the first time I was sent out of school to an external meeting, I felt so important. Feeling a bit peckish, I took the opportunity to eat a cereal bar on the way. I enjoyed the meeting and left feeling I had represented my school well. As I adjusted the car's mirror to drive back to school, horror struck: in the middle of my chin was a large, melted chocolate chip! All my hopes of having made a good impression faded.

When Paul talks about restoring people 'gently' and 'watching [ourselves] or [we] also may be tempted' (v. 1), it reminds me of the chocolate chip incident. I mustn't be so busy looking for 'sawdust' in my fellow believer's eye that I don't notice the 'plank' in my own (Matthew 7:3–5) – or the chocolate chip on my chin! I need to respond to the prompting of the Holy Spirit in my own life to convict me of sin before I start pointing it out in others.

It's hard, sometimes, to keep having the grace to love and serve others in all their flawed, human glory – and it might be hard for others to do the same for us! But Paul encourages us not to 'become weary in doing good' because the 'harvest' it will lead to will be more than worth the efforts we have made (v. 9).

Again, though, it is important to keep reinforcing Paul's message – he isn't interested in outward, rule-driven behaviour or performance. He wants to see a community of believers using their Christ-given freedom to serve one another well, with gentleness and kindness, encouraging one another to live well from a place of grace.

Ask God today to help you to face the reality of your own sin and flaws. Thank him for his forgiveness and grace. Ask him to help you treat those around you with the same grace and kindness.

GEORGIE TENNANT

Outward show or inward authenticity?

Neither circumcision nor uncircumcision means anything; what counts is the new creation. (v. 15, NIV)

When my oldest son was little, he fell into our neighbour's pond. It was so covered in algae that it looked like an extension of the grass he'd just been playing on. He soon found out that the grassy appearance hid the reality beneath and plunged into the cold water. My neighbour and I dragged him, spluttering and shocked, back to the safety of dry ground. The pond's appearance deceived him initially, but the truth hidden beneath it soon became painfully apparent.

This is the message Paul drives home in the final section of his letter, reinforcing one last time the key theme he has expounded throughout: that plastering on a Christian veneer will not change your life or the lives of others around you. It might be convincing for a while, but it soon leads down into cold, murky depths. Simply keeping up appearances leads only to misery and slavery, not freedom. Outward show means nothing. Only deep, inner heart change truly matters and that happens through God's work in us, not our own efforts to try harder. What a great relief to us all! It isn't about us. On our own, we wouldn't get very far. It is only God's grace that can transform us from the inside out.

What have you learnt as we have journeyed though Galatians? I hope reading it with new eyes has ignited a fresh excitement in your heart for God's outrageous grace. What have you let go of and laid down as you have relinquished performance and received more grace? Be sure to stay free in the days and weeks that follow, not letting a 'gospel-plus' mentality creep insidiously back in. Go and live free, passing on this incredible message of grace to those around you.

Spend time today thanking God afresh for the grace given freely to you, through Jesus. Ask for his help not to fall back into the bondage of a performance, 'gospel-plus' mindset as you go forward.

GEORGIE TENNANT

To order

Online: **brfonline.org.uk**
Telephone: **+44 (0)1865 319700**
Mon–Fri 9.30–17.00

Delivery times within the UK are normally 15 working days. Prices are correct at the time of going to press but may change without prior notice.

Title	Price	Qty	Total
Day by Day with God (Jan–Apr 2026) – single copy	£5.25		
Day by Day with God (May–Aug 2026) – single copy	£5.99		
An A–Z of Parenting for Faith	£12.99		
Reflected in Nature	£14.99		
This Crown of Comfort	£9.99		

POSTAGE AND PACKING CHARGES			
Order value	**UK**	**Europe**	**Rest of world**
Under £7.00	£2.00	Available on request	Available on request
£7.00–£29.99	£3.00		
£30.00 and over	FREE		

Total value of books	
Donation	
Postage and packing	
Total for this order	

Please complete in BLOCK CAPITALS

Title ________ First name/initials ________________ Surname ____________________________

Address ____

____ Postcode ____________

Acc. No. ______________________ Telephone ______________________________

Email ____

Method of payment

❑ Cheque (made payable to BRF) ❑ MasterCard / Visa

Card no. ☐☐☐☐ ☐☐☐☐ ☐☐☐☐ ☐☐☐☐

Expires end M M Y Y

We will use your personal data to process this order. From time to time we may send you information about the work of BRF Ministries. Please contact us if you wish to discuss your mailing preferences. Our privacy possible is available at **brf.org.uk/privacy.**

Registered with FUNDRAISING REGULATOR

Please return this form to:

BRF Ministries, 15 The Chambers, Vineyard, Abingdon OX14 3FE | **enquiries@brf.org.uk**

For terms and cancellation information, please visit **brfonline.org.uk/terms.**

Bible Reading Fellowship (BRF) is a charity (233280) and company limited by guarantee (301324), registered in England and Wales

SUBSCRIPTION INFORMATION

Each issue of ***Day by Day with God*** is available from Christian bookshops everywhere. Copies may also be available through your church book agent or from the person who distributes Bible reading notes in your church.

Alternatively, you may obtain ***Day by Day with God*** on subscription direct from the publisher. There are two kinds of subscription:

Individual subscription
covering 3 issues for 4 copies or less, payable in advance (including postage & packing).

To order, please complete the details on page 144 and return with the appropriate payment to: BRF Ministries, 15 The Chambers, Vineyard, Abingdon OX14 3FE

You can also use the form on page 144 to order a gift subscription for a friend.

Group subscription
covering 3 issues for 5 copies or more, sent to one UK address (post free).

Please note that the annual billing period for group subscriptions runs from 1 May to 30 April.

To order, please complete the details on page 143 and return with the appropriate payment to: BRF Ministries, 15 The Chambers, Vineyard, Abingdon OX14 3FE

You will receive an invoice with the first issue of notes.

All our Bible reading notes can be ordered online by visiting
brfonline.org.uk/collections/subscriptions

All subscription enquiries should be directed to:
BRF Ministries, 15 The Chambers, Vineyard, Abingdon OX14 3FE
+44 (0)1865 319700 | enquiries@brf.org.uk

DAY BY DAY WITH GOD GROUP SUBSCRIPTION FORM

To set up a recurring subscription, please go to **brfonline.org.uk/subscriptions**

The group subscription rate for ***Day by Day with God*** will be £17.97 per person until April 2027.

☐ I would like to take out a group subscription for __________ (quantity) copies.

☐ Please start my order with the May 2026 / September 2026 / January 2027 * issue. I would like to pay annually/receive an invoice* with each edition of the notes. (**delete as appropriate*)

Please do not send any money with your order. Send your order to BRF Ministries and we will send you an invoice.

Name and address of the person organising the group subscription:

Title __________ First name/initials ______________ Surname ______________________________

Address ____

____ Postcode ________________

Telephone ___________________________ Email ______________________________________

Church ____

Name and address of the person paying the invoice if the invoice needs to be sent directly to them:

Title __________ First name/initials ______________ Surname ______________________________

Address ____

____ Postcode ________________

Telephone ___________________________ Email ______________________________________

We will use your personal data to process this order. From time to time we may send you information about the work of BRF Ministries. Please contact us if you wish to discuss your mailing preferences. Our privacy policy is available at **brf.org.uk/privacy.**

Please return this form to:

BRF Ministries, 15 The Chambers, Vineyard, Abingdon OX14 3FE

enquiries@brf.org.uk

For terms and cancellation information, please visit **brfonline.org.uk/terms.**

DAY BY DAY WITH GOD INDIVIDUAL/GIFT SUBSCRIPTION FORM

To order online, please visit **brfonline.org.uk/subscriptions**

☐ I would like to give a gift subscription (please provide both names and addresses)

☐ I would like to take out a subscription myself (complete your name and address details only once)

Title __________ First name/initials ______________ Surname ________________________________

Address ____

____ Postcode ______________________

Telephone ____________________________ Email ____

Gift subscription name ____

Gift subscription address ____

____ Postcode ______________________

Gift subscription (20 words max. or include your own gift card):

____

____

Please send *Day by Day with God* beginning with the May 2026 / September 2026 / January 2027 issue (*delete as appropriate*):

(*please tick box*)	**UK**	**Europe**	**Rest of world**
1-year subscription	☐ £25.20	☐ £37.50	☐ £44.25

Optional donation to support the work of BRF Ministries £ __________________

Total enclosed £ __________________ (cheques should be made payable to 'BRF')

Please charge my MasterCard / Visa with £ _________________

Card no. ☐☐☐☐ ☐☐☐☐ ☐☐☐☐ ☐☐☐☐

Expires end M M Y Y

We will use your personal data to process this order. From time to time we may send you information about the work of BRF Ministries. Please contact us if you wish to discuss your mailing preferences. Our privacy policy is available at **brf.org.uk/privacy.**

Please return this form to:

BRF Ministries, 15 The Chambers, Vineyard, Abingdon OX14 3FE

enquiries@brf.org.uk

For terms and cancellation information, please visit **brfonline.org.uk/terms**.

Bible Reading Fellowship is a charity (233280) and company limited by guarantee (301324), registered in England and Wales